Meet Me at Kay's

Meet Me at

A Celebration of
Ray's Place in
Kent, Ohio

Patrick J. O'Connor

Black Squirrel Books™

An imprint of The Kent State University Press
Kent, Ohio 44242 www.KentStateUniversityPress.com

Black Squirrel Books™

Frisky, industrious black squirrels are a familiar sight on the Kent State University campus and the inspiration for Black Squirrel Books™, a trade imprint of The Kent State University Press. www.KentStateUniversityPress.com

A portion of the proceeds from the sale of *Meet Me at Ray's* supports the Ray's Place Entrepreneurship Scholarship in Kent State University's College of Business Administration.

Library of Congress Cataloging-in-Publication Data
O'Connor, Patrick J. (Patrick James), 1950–
  Meet me at Ray's : a celebration of Ray's Place in Kent, Ohio / Patrick J. O'Connor.
    pages cm
  ISBN 978-1-60635-173-4 (paperback) ∞
1. Ray's Place (Kent, Ohio) 2. Restaurants—Ohio—Kent—History. 3. Bars (Drinking establishments)—Ohio—Kent—History. 4. Sports—Social aspects—Ohio—Kent—History. 5. College students—Ohio—Kent—Social life and customs. 6. Kent (Ohio)—Social life and customs. 7. Kent (Ohio)—Biography. I. Title.
  TX945.5.R39O25 2013
  647.95771'37—dc23
                                                  2012048530

17 16 15 14 13   5 4 3 2 1

To the many loyal customers,
employees, owners, vendors, and friends
of Ray's Place since 1937

Contents

Illustrations

Foreword

CHARLIE THOMAS '74

On Sunday evening, December 12, 1978, the previous owners of Ray's Place and I had just completed taking inventory of stock and supplies since I was taking over the following day. As we were preparing to leave, Buddy LoCicero, one of the owners, said, "You probably want to stay and let this all sink in. When we bought the place, we just sat here and couldn't believe it was ours." I said, "No, I have a feeling I'm going to be spending a lot of time here." And so, the journey began!

From the very beginning, all I did was work, because I knew that was what it was going to take to make the place successful. One of the first things I did was call a meeting with what were now my employees and lay the foundation for the future of Ray's Place. I told them I was eliminating the drink tokens. The previous owners had rewarded employees for working a shift by giving them tokens that could be redeemed for drinks. I told them, "No more tokens," which, needless to say, went over like a lead balloon. Under the previous owners, when the late-night shift was over, the employees had to stay to mop the floors and clean the establishment. I told them, "Starting today, when you finish your late-night shift, you will no longer have to stay and clean the place, and I'm giving everyone a raise." That was a crowd pleaser and really helped with taking away the tokens. I then proceeded to explain the Ray's Place success equation:

Ray's Place = the customer + employee + physical plant

I explained why the customer was first in the equation and how the employee is so important to the business. Finally, I explained where the physical plant, meaning the building, equipment, furniture, pictures, and the like, fit into the scheme of things. To finish, I laid out the three

Ray's Place commandments:

1. Thou shall not steal.
2. Thou shall not knowingly serve someone under age.
3. Thou shall not drink on the job.

This started my ownership of Ray's Place and set the stage for how it was going to proceed in the future. I knew from the start that I was going to have to practice what I was preaching . . . that I would have to do everything I expected of the employees. I realized early on that Ray's Place was much larger than me. It takes a lot of good people to make Ray's the place it is. I'm sure that each of the previous owners realized that the customer is everything, because without the customer a business is nothing.

Ray's Place has changed many times throughout the years, but each time the customer was first and foremost in the thought process. I like to say that Ray's Place is always changing but it remains the same. It is like an old shoe: it's comfortable, it stretches, it bends, but it is stable.

Would you buy a Mo-Fo from this man? Charles Ray "Charlie" Thomas in 1979. Photo courtesy of Charlie Thomas.

Preface

Seventy-five years is a long time, unless you're referring to oceans or mountains. It's an especially long time in the life of a small business. Lots of things can happen over the decades: changes in customer tastes and preferences, financial struggles, economic downturns, competition, government regulation, and just plain fate can bounce a small business around like a beach ball. It's a major accomplishment to weather the various storms that can rage over the years. Yet in a small college town in Ohio, one business stands out among others that have faced these storms.

About 50 bars in Kent, Ohio, have come and gone while one endures. Ray's Place celebrated three-quarters of a century in business in 2012, which gave me the idea of writing this book.

For the last 25 years I have enjoyed going to Ray's Place. I've gone with friends, colleagues, family members, and sometimes just by myself. And in my travels, if I wore anything to identify myself with Kent State University, strangers would frequently strike up conversations that related to Ray's. The more I went to Ray's, the more curious I became as to how this one business could have such an amazing following of customers. I also began to notice that the same employees were there, year after year. Having a bit of a business background myself, I was curious about the unique ways the business operated and how it has lasted so long. I listened as customers talked about their affection for Ray's Place, especially during Kent State University's Homecoming celebrations when that affection was at its peak.

It occurred to me that just about every customer and employee had a special memory or story about why they loved Ray's Place. It was then that I began to think that a collection of their stories and experiences would make for some entertaining and interesting reading, something I've been interested in for years.

As I wrote this book I was asked by many people what kind of book it would be. Would it be a business book, a history book, a nostalgia book, or maybe an entrepreneurial story? I thought to myself, it will be a bit of all those things, but mainly it will be a book celebrating the almost eight decades of a unique business with unbreakable bonds to the city of Kent and Kent State University, one that holds a special place in the lives of the folks who eat and drink, play and work, gather and celebrate there. And it would be told through the memories and experiences of those people. It would be unlike any book I'd ever written, and that excited me. It would be an "organic" book because it would be rooted in the hearts, minds, and experiences of the people who know it best: the customers and employees.

So here is *Meet Me at Ray's: A Celebration of Ray's Place in Kent, Ohio*. It features the history, stories, memories, and experiences of the customers and employees who have made Ray's what it is, from 1937 to the present day. To complement their stories, I have included photographs from years past and commissioned some new ones, too, and proceeds from the book sales supports a scholarship in the KSU School of Business.

I hope that *Meet Me at Ray's* provides insight into why so many people are loyal to Ray's Place. You may laugh at times, reflect at other times, and maybe have a few nostalgic moments of your own. I also hope you will get a sense of what makes some places special and how important that is to us.

There were many wonderful moments in writing this book. Most of them began when I opened an e-mail and started to read a story or memory of a customer or employee. Each e-mail was special and took me to a place I never could have imagined (and I have a pretty active imagination). I enjoyed meeting all sorts of people as a result of the new places this book has taken me. The process of reading and gathering these Ray's Place stories was an adventure of its own with its own energy, a truly unique and amazing experience! I hope it is also a unique and amazing experience for you.

Patrick J. O'Connor
Edisto Beach, SC
Kent, Ohio

Acknowledgments

There are many people to acknowledge for their participation in *Meet Me at Ray's*. I appreciate the input and support I have received from my colleagues at Kent State University: Kevin Brozien, Foluke Omuson, Jason Prufer, and Nancy Schiappa. Thanks also to Sandy and Harry Halem of the Kent Historical Society and to Will Underwood and the personnel at Kent State University Press/Black Squirrel Books.™

I thank my wife, Sue O'Connor, for the idea of a competition to decide the book title and for her continued support and patience; son Patrick for the artwork; daughter Erin for the manuscript research assistance; and sons Sean and Ryan for reviewing the manuscript. We received 29 suggestions for the book title, so thank you to everyone who submitted—but a special thanks to Mike Kaschak and Dan Karp who submitted the winning title. Thanks also to John Jewell, PhD (KSU, '98) for manuscript feedback. I appreciate all the information and encouragement from the Flogge family, especially from Al Flogge. Thanks to Mikala Pritts of MP Photos for the original photography and to Beth Benjamin for IT services and support. And finally, to Ray's Place owner Charlie Thomas and the many friends, customers, and employees of Ray's Place—my heartfelt thanks! Your experiences have been the true inspiration that became *Meet Me at Ray's*.

AUTHOR NOTE TO READERS:

Meet Me at Ray's consists primarily of stories from the experiences of customers and employees. The contributer is identified after each story. Readers will also see phrases quoted in our waitress illustration. These phrases are actual slogans used at Ray's over the years. Also, the comments in "Charlie Says" are actual statements made by Charlie Thomas related to various events that occured at Ray's. Finally, a number of trivia questions related to Ray's Place are sprinkled throughout the book. Answers to the questions can be found in the book.

Meet Me at Ray's

Original three-story building now occupied by Ray's Place ca. 1898. The man standing in front is Hale Thompson whose family owned a drugstore in Kent, Ohio, for over 100 years. Photo courtesy of the Kent Historical Society.

 # The Players

You need a scorecard to know the players associated with Ray's Place. Here is a short list of the key people:

Ray Salitore—the original Ray and owner from 1937 to 1945
Margie Salitore—married to Ray Salitore
Rocco (aka Rocky or Rock) and Andy Flogge—brothers who bought Ray's Place from Ray Salitore; owners from 1945 to 1975
Verna Flogge—married to Andy
Albert Flogge—youngest of the nine Flogge children
Charles Flogge (aka Uncle Charley)—Rocky and Andy's brother; built the original booths at Ray's Place and installed TV in 1946
Tom Shaw, Buddy, and Mary LoCicero—the third owners, from 1975 to 1978
Charlie Thomas (aka Stereo Chuck)—the fourth and current owner since 1978
Vanetta Gritton (aka Gertie)—worked for the four owners of Ray's Place for 40 years; the chili at Ray's is named for her
The Ray's Gang, The Mooseherd, The Ruggers, The Collegiates, The Yanks—groups of college students that have aligned themselves with Ray's over the years

Story contributors in *Meet Me at Ray's* are cited as follows:

(Name of contributor)—employee or customer submitting the story about Ray's
(Year)—indicates the graduation year(s) if contributor is a KSU alumnus. For example, "(Ash, '60, '61)" refers to Charles Ash, KSU alum in 1960 and 1961.
(Anon)—indicates contributor wished to remain anonymous

Kent mayor Jerry Fiala designated Friday, September 14, 2012, as "Ray's Place Day" in Kent, issuing a proclamation recognizing the 75th anniversary of the restaurant.

Hi, Welcome to Ray's Place

· ·

It was December 9th, 1991, when I opened that wooden door and it was as if time stood still. It seemed like the voices and music stopped as my eyes connected with a guy across the bar. Several hours later I realized he was next to me at the bar. The rest is history. I don't remember how the conversation started, but I knew this was the love of my life. He proposed the following May and we were married in December 1992. Every year on December 9th we return to Ray's and sit on "our" bar stools (second and third from the door). Each time I open that wooden door and see those Christmas bulbs hanging from the ceiling, it seems like time stands still again. *(Morgan, '90)*

Colleen Morgan and her husband Eric are one of many couples who found their future at Ray's Place.

IN THE BEGINNING

It was 1937. The war in Europe was heating up while most of America was still reeling from the Great Depression. Blues pioneer Robert Johnson had just written "Sweet Home Chicago," the New York Yankees won another world series, and the Golden Gate Bridge was opened for traffic. Disney's *Snow White and the Seven Dwarfs* was released, the Hindenburg exploded, Amelia Earhart and Fred Noonan disappeared, and Martin L. Davey, from Kent, was governor of Ohio. Small towns all across the country were seeing their landscape and social fabric change. Railroads would soon lose their dominant place in American life. And Kent, Ohio, would begin its slow evolution from a town dominated by the railroad to one dominated by a university.

It may seem like an odd time to have opened a restaurant, given all the changes that were occurring. But Ray Salitore, a son of Italian immigrants, decided to do just that. Just as millions of other first-generation Americans did, he decided to become an entrepreneur. He wanted to earn his share of the American Dream. Although the American Dream is an often-used phrase, most people are unsure of its actual meaning.

In 1931, at the height of the Great Depression, historian James Adams defined it as "where life should be better, richer and fuller for everyone with opportunity to each according to ability and achievement." Ray Salitore wanted to pursue this dream by opening Ray's Place.

A pretty amazing place: Ray's Place in Kent, Ohio. It's been serving up food, beverages, and fun on the banks of the Cuyahoga River for more than 75 years. Among other descriptions, Ray's has been referred to as the place "where hustlers meet to hustle the hustlers" and where "they welcome business people, students, garbage collectors, janitors, and rock 'n' rollers in general." The popularity of Ray's Place hit the national stage in 2011 when Iron Chef Michael Symon declared a Ray's burger to be his favorite. "It's a classic," he said on his Food Network television show in reference to the venerable Mo-Fo double-burger. The experiences and memories of customers and employees tell the colorful story of this classic place.

Ray Salitore and his wife, Margie, at the Ray's Place back entrance, a common scene from 1937 to 1946. Photo courtesy of Charlie Thomas.

Seen from Franklin Avenue and looking again much as it did in 1937, the front of Ray's Place is pictured in its 75th anniversary year in 2012. Photo courtesy of Charlie Thomas.

Ray's Around the World

Ray's has seven imported beers on draft and 70 in bottles. Photo by Mikala Pritts.

Prior to the ownership by the LoCiceros and Tom Shaw in the mid-1970s, Ray's Place had featured mostly domestic beer in bottles. This owner group thought Kent was ripe for some new tastes in beer. As with other firsts at Ray's, it was a pretty big risk. No one was entirely sure how local citizens would react to international import beers. Plus, many students might shy away from the higher price of the imports. But they forged ahead anyway, bringing in draft import beers such Heineken, Guinness, Labatt's, and others. As it turned out, the idea was a hit, especially among locals and professors. The owners even created a carryout special called an "Around the World," which featured a 12-pack of various international bottled beers. Also, international faculty members visiting KSU were enthused, as Dr. Joe Diestel's story indicates:

Members of KSU's Math Department have many memories of Ray's. Beginning in 1973, the Math Department hosted international conferences that were attended by folks from every continent and many countries. Now, when most mathematicians from around the globe come to any meeting in Kent, on arrival they often head down to Ray's to locate other old friends, knowing Ray's is the place. It's likely that most abstract mathematical analysts in the West have spent a few enjoyable hours supping at Ray's, and many return whenever the occasion to do so arises." (Diestel, emeritus professor of math)

Apparently, many international guests like Ray's because they can obtain their favorite "local" brew. As of this writing, Ray's has 77 foreign beers available on most any day: seven on draft and 70 in bottles. An early Ray's menu lists beers from the following countries: Japan, Italy, Mexico, Norway, Poland, Switzerland, Holland, Finland, Canada, England, Ireland, Australia, Czechoslovakia, and Brazil. In 2013, Ray's offered a total of 224 beers on tap or in bottle.

Ray's basement with kegs. This is where the pour begins. Photo by Mikala Pritts.

Ohio's First Sports Bar

Ray's Place is considered to be one of the first bars to televise sporting events in the United States. In 1946, Ray's acquired the first commercial television in Portage County, Ohio, as reported in the *Record-Courier*. Sixty-seven years later, in April 2013, the Ohio Licensed Beverage Association honored Ray's as the first sports bar in Ohio, a fitting distinction. Ray's may also be the first bar in the United States to televise sports.

• •

I distinctly remember watching Satchel Paige pitch for Cleveland, and he was brought to the Tribe in 1948. I graduated in 1950, so I know Ray's had TV before then, because I watched it there. *(Bob West, emeritus professor of journalism)*

Television first came to Ray's in 1946 when avid sports fans Rocky and Andy had their brother Charlie set up a black-and-white television in the bar. The brand was a Muntz, named after pioneering industrialist Earl Muntz from California. Muntz was nicknamed "Madman" because of his peculiar ways and innovative ideas.

It was common in the early years of television for patrons to visit Ray's Place to watch sporting events since most people didn't have television at home. Rocky commented in a newspaper story that "no one had television in their homes and people went crazy to come down to see this big TV set and watch Wednesday and Friday night boxing and wrestling." And Ray's was host to numerous KSU coaches who showed game films on Sunday afternoons. Even a major league umpire, Bill McKinley, would show films of World Series baseball games. Sometimes a famous athlete, such as the golfer in the story below, would stop in at Ray's just like any other patron.

• •

One evening, Rocky approached me with that "wide as the world" smile he had. Tagging along was a familiar face, but I couldn't put a name to it, a tallish guy with a friendly face. Rocky's mission that moment was to introduce me to this gentleman, who stuck out a welcoming hand even before the

Television At Ray's Place

The first commercial television set in Portage county has been installed at Ray's Place, 135 Franklin ave., Kent.

The set, a United States Television Company product, is ideally situated in the bar and dining room. The bottom of the 19 by 26 inch screen, the largest obtainable at the present time, is six feet from the floor, thus providing an unobstructed view of the entire set from any place in the room. The set is encased in a maroon-colored imitation leather case. Reception, both in sound and vision, has been very nearly perfect to date.

Although WEWS, Cleveland's television station has not as yet scheduled commercial broadcasting, patrons of Ray's Place have witnessed excellent reception of daily impromptu broadcasts. Included in regular current afternoon and evening programs have been basketball games, musical programs, news broadcasts, interviews and most other usual radio broadcasts.

The present non-commercial schedule on which WEWS operates may be found daily on the radio page of the Cleveland Plain Dealer. Future plans at WEWS call for the televising of most major sports events in Cleveland as well as many other general programs of public interest.

Among the surrounding radio stations showing interest and planning for television is station WAKR in Akron. A definite date has not yet been set for the incorporating of television into any one of several interested stations but the specifically mentioned WAKR seems to be the farthest advanced.

"Rocky" and "Andy" Flogg, co-owners of Ray's Place invite one and all to spend an evening at their restaurant-bar where you can witness your favorite programs by television while you enjoy the very best in food and drink. The picture shows the set with "Rocky" on the left and "Andy" on the right.

In 1946 the *Daily Kent Courier-Tribune* featured this article about the first commercial television in Portage County, Ohio. The television made Ray's one of the first bars in the country to televise sporting events. Photo courtesy of the *Record-Courier*.

greeting. Smiling hugely as always, Rocky said: "Ken, meet Noel Blankenship, a young professor at KSU; Noel, meet Ken Venturi." I had no idea that Ken Venturi was the subject of one of golf's famous TV moments in which he staggered with heat exhaustion, to the cheers of the gallery, up the last fairway to win one of golf's most famous tournaments. I was probably the only person in the bar who would've asked, "What do you do, Ken?" He said, with his amiable smile, 'I'm a golfer.'" *(Blankenship, emeritus professor of technology)*

1. Who came up with the idea of the shot wheel?

9

Ken Venturi won the United States Open golf championship and was PGA Player of the Year in 1964.

· ·

On many summer afternoons when the New York Yankees were in Cleveland, Phil "The Scooter" Rizutto, the retired Yankee shortstop and the Yankee broadcaster at the time, would come down to Kent with several other baseball players to play golf with Rocky. When the Cleveland Browns were in summer training camp at Hiram College, many players would come to Ray's in the evening. Pro bowlers from Akron were also often seen there. I don't think any other bar in the area could boast such a clientele. *(Ash, '61 and '62)*

In addition to numerous famous professional athletes who visited Ray's, students, both in high school and college, frequently enjoyed watching sporting events at Ray's as the following stories indicate.

· ·

In the early '90s, my two girlfriends and I were big Cleveland Cavaliers fans. We would come up to Ray's to watch most games. In fact, most of the bartenders would see us walk in and ask us what channel the game was on, so they could put it on for us! At the time, one of our favorite players was not a starter. He only got in if the Cavs were way up or way down. But every time Bobby Phills got in the game, we all had to do a shot of Tequila. That was a lot of fun . . . until he started playing a lot more often. Good thing we always walked to Ray's! *(Nielsen)*

My most vivid memory about Ray's was back in 1979 when my girlfriends and I were there as immature seniors from Green High School. Brian Sipe from the Cleveland Browns was there, and one of my friends pushed me right into him. It was very embarrassing. (He was very cute, though.) Ray's T-shirts were popular back then, and of course I purchased one because at the time, the guy I was dating was named Ray. I have been to Ray's since for lunch and dinner with my daughter who graduated from Kent State in 2012. *(Kapper)*

We've spent endless hours watching the Indians, the Cavs, the Golden Flashes, the Ohio State Buckeyes, and many more of our favorite sports teams at Ray's. It's so much fun when the whole place is having a great time, clapping and yelling at the TV and giving high fives to everyone around them. A particular time I will never forget was Game 6 of the 1997 World Series. The Tribe was playing the Florida Marlins in Florida. The series was Florida up three games to Cleveland's two games. It was Halloween weekend in downtown Kent. We went to Ray's early to watch the game and have dinner before the crowds got too crazy. A crowd favorite, Omar

Rocky Flogge, left, with his father, Joe, and Yogi Berra at Cleveland Stadium in the 1950s. The Flogges were friends with many professional athletes. Photo courtesy of Al Flogge.

Vizquel, dove for a ball, sprang to his feet, and hurled a perfect strike to the first baseman! The Ray's crowd erupted like I've never seen before. I felt the floors actually shaking! The Tribe evened the series 3–3 and headed into Game 7 of the World Series! We all know the heartbreaking end to that series. *(Duffy, '74)*

Many high-profile sports figures were associated with Ray's Place over the years. Actually, Rocky and Andy Flogge were personal friends with baseball players Yogi Berra and Gene Michael (who played at Kent State University where the baseball field is named after him). The Flogges were also good friends with storied football coach Lou Holtz, who began his career playing at KSU. Other KSU athletes who visited Ray's and went on to success in the sports world include baseball players Rich Rollins, Thurman Munson, and Steve Stone; football players Nick Saban, Gary Pinkel, Jack Lambert, Gerald Tinker, Josh Cribbs, and Antonio Gates; and golfer Ben Curtis, winner of the British Open in 2003.

• •

Ray's was my regular watering hole for watching sports. I think I watched every Monday night football game there from 1970 to 1972. *(Taylor, '72)*

Let the good times roll

Special Events at Ray's

Ray's has been the go-to place for special celebrations in Kent since it opened. Twenty-first birthday celebrations head the list. Returning customers have also gathered each year to celebrate St. Patrick's Day, graduations, Homecoming, and Halloween.

21ST BIRTHDAY CELEBRATIONS

Ray's has long been a hot spot for people to celebrate their birthdays, especially the 21st. Customers who present the proper identification to indicate it's their birthday receive a spin on Ray's famous shot wheel.

A common occurrence is to see a group of young people, often college students, stepping up to the bar for the 21st birthday rite of passage. The group directs the initiate to the bartender, who takes over the honors. The birthday celebrant spins the arrow on the shot wheel and receives a complimentary beverage wherever the arrow lands. The wheel features options for drinks with names such as "Sex on the Beach," "Bloody Brains," "Sexy Alligator," and "Bartender's Choice." Surprisingly, there is no option for the "Futher Mucker." This popular, signature drink, a citrus-based concoction, has been a favorite at Ray's Place for almost 40 years. More on this drink later.

It's interesting to note the number of customers who shared stories referring to their first legal drink on their 21st birthday at Ray's. Here are a few samples of 21st birthday celebrations at Ray's:

· ·

At the stroke of midnight on January 26th, 2012, I began my 21st birthday celebrations with a shot at Ray's bar. Ever since freshman year, I knew that this day would come, and the only place a good Kent Stater should indulge in their first legal beverage is Ray's Place! *(Kalar, '12)*

· ·

My first memory of Ray's Place was on my 21st birthday when bartender BJ gave me a "Sweaty Mexican," which promptly sent me to hug the tree outside. A few weeks later I applied to work there, and that is where the real journey began. *(Kugelman)*

As a KSU student, I enjoyed many evenings at Ray's Place and remember celebrating my 21st birthday there with friends. The food was always great and a treat for a college student. But let's be honest . . . we went for the beer! *(Whitworth, '79)*

Some students look forward to celebrating that milestone 21st birthday as a family tradition, as the following stories indicate.

I absolutely love Ray's Place. It has become my favorite restaurant on the planet because of their fabulous veggie pita and garden burger. The laid-back atmosphere at Ray's Place adds even more to the experience. Ray's Place has been a favorite in my family for decades. I can't wait to spin the wheel on my 21st birthday. *(Miller)*

Both of my parents graduated from Kent State. In 1976 my dad celebrated his 21st birthday at Ray's Place. Many years down the road in 2009, I turned 21. My family came down to celebrate it with me at Ray's Place. We had two generations celebrating their 21st birthday at Ray's Place. *(Campobenedetto, '11)*

I'm a lifelong Kent resident. My family has had numerous enjoyable experiences at Ray's Place. We dine at Ray's several times a month. Not only did I celebrate my 21st birthday in Ray's but I got to celebrate my wife's and my three boys' 21st birthdays at Ray's and spin the wheel. *(Lewis)*

This international student had quite a celebration on his first birthday in the United States. His friends took him to Ray's for a surprise birthday he'll remember for life.

It was my 23rd birthday and first in the United States. Two of my friends and I went to the MAC Center to watch basketball game first. All of my friends said they were busy so they could not be with me. I could understand because they all were students. I and my two friends, Amanda and Axel, went back to our dorm after basketball game, and they said, "We three should go to the Ray's Place to celebrate your birthday!" So we walked toward the Ray's Place. Ten minutes later we got to the Ray's

Place. Axel had problem with entering the bar because he has German driver license. (They were really strict of checking ID, and German licenses sometimes were not accepted.) We three went into the restaurant and were searching for the seats available. It was crowded as usual. Suddenly, many people in the bar started howling and I saw a cake. I thought "What is that?" and ignored them. Then someone shouted, "John!" (My baptism name that all of my friends call me.) It was my friends' surprise birthday party for me. I almost cried for that and really surprised. Almost every people in the bar started singing birthday song for me kindly. It was the best memory with best food for me. *(Kim)*

· ·

I have many fond memories of Ray's Place with Mary in the kitchen and Jan out front. This was the first, and perhaps the only, time I celebrated my birthday with cake and beer! *(DeGiroloma)*

· ·

In the late '60s, while in high school, we'd visit the upstairs of Ray's, which, at the time, was Johnny's pool hall. After spending a few hours there we'd visit Ray's. We did this so often we became known as semi-regulars. I looked old for my age and was never carded. I remember the surprised looks when I pulled out my license when I was finally legal. *(Schnee)*

· ·

I did my undergrad at Bowling Green State University, and the guy I was dating at the time went to Kent State. I visited often and Ray's was where he took me to have my first legal beer on my 21st birthday. (We came back several times after that.) Who knew that four years later I'd be a Golden Flash and my boyfriend's stomping ground would become my stomping ground? *(D'Abate)*

· ·

2. Who came up with the name for the Futher Mucker drink?

Some things in life are meant to be remembered. My son purchased his first legal beers (for me and him) on his 21st birthday at Ray's. My daughter, whose birthday is on New Year's Day, spent New Year's Eve with me so that she could purchase her first legal beer for her old man. *(Hostler, '99; Mike Hostler has played the bagpipes at Ray's on St. Patrick's Day for many years)*

ST. PATRICK'S DAY

3. Who named the Mo-Fo ?

My parents have taken me to Ray's Place ever since I could walk. I remember going there on St. Patrick's Day and always getting a green Sprite. It was the highlight of my year at Ray's (along with visiting the pinball machines), and I looked forward to it every year. Now I can look forward to going in someday and getting a green beer and continuing to forever be a loving customer of Ray's Place. *(Meindl)*

I was all about getting into where I couldn't. I had been using a fake ID in Kent since I was a KSU freshman. Mostly I would use it at the Brewhouse or clubs, but on St. Patrick's Day of my junior year I was feeling risky and tipsy. My friends wanted to go to Ray's Place . . . my attempt to get in wasn't so successful. There I was, drunk and alone on St. Patrick's Day, because I lost my friends. I still have no idea how I found my way home. I anticipated the day I turned 21, so I could finally enjoy Ray's Place. *(Janet B.)*

During a particularly rowdy St. Patrick's Day at Ray's, my friends and I were enjoying drinks and laughs at the upstairs bar. An inebriated acquaintance of ours spotted us and stumbled over to our table to chat. Out of nowhere he proclaimed, "I will buy ALL of you a round of Guinness if you shake my hand!" We were skeptical, but all nine of us shook his hand—and sure enough, nine pints of Guinness found their way to our table. Needless to say we toasted our friend that round! *(Schlosser, '10)*

HALLOWEEN

Halloween 2009: my sorority sister Julie and I walked into Ray's dressed as gladiators from the movie *300*. While drinking my Strongbow and getting hit on by Harry Potter, some guy I had never seen before came up to save me; he was dressed as a tool from *Tool Academy*. The rest is history, and we just got our first house together. Mike claims that I was checking him out in the huge mirror behind the bar all night long and decided to approach me since I was interested. Later I pointed out to him there is no huge mirror behind the bar, and he was either already too far gone to realize this or used it as his excuse to talk to me.

Mike came up and asked if I wanted to take a shot with him, and while he was waiting to order, he stood next to me on the opposite side of Harry Potter. It made it easy to turn my back to the other guy and start talking to Mike. His pickup line was something like, "Where are you from?" We learned we grew up about five minutes away from each other and had a lot of mutual friends (he was in a band with a guy whose little sister was my friend in high school), but somehow we'd never met. In true bar fashion, his number was saved in my phone that night as "Mike Halloween," and I don't think I replaced it with his real last name for about a year. The best part was we were both happy at Ray's that night and snapped a picture of the two of us, so now we have a picture from the very first time we met, and I am holding the tool sign that reads "COMMITMENT." If only he had known then! *(Ahlers, '11)*

Way to go, Mike!

HOMECOMING

Homecoming has always been huge at Ray's. I think more people come back to see Ray's than to see KSU. One year the bar was so packed, wall to wall, no room to walk, and the song "Jump Around," from House of Pain, came on the jukebox (which, by the way, is the unofficial anthem for Ray's). The crowd went crazy, we cranked the stereo, and everyone started jumping in unison. The entire back bar started to move, cooler doors shaking, and the Budweiser horse light moving. We all looked at each other wondering if we should stop the jumping. Then the old T-shirt rack started to sway back and forth. It was perched up above the old cooler near the door and was about to come down (10 to 16 feet high). With two helping hands, I climbed up the cooler and stabilized the rack from tipping over into the crowded back bar area. We let the music play, and it was an awesome night. *(Levicki)*

As a further testament to the bond between Ray's Place and collegiate life, Charlie Thomas was named Grand Marshal of the KSU Homecoming Parade for 2013.

Usually occurring in October, Kent State University's Homecoming is the busiest day of the year at Ray's Place. Photo courtesy of Charlie Thomas.

Every year at Homecoming, 500 commemorative pint glasses are passed out to customers.

GRADUATION CELEBRATIONS

. . . .

I spent many weekends at Ray's during my time at Kent State University. It is a wonderful place to gather with friends and family. I was so fond of Ray's that my whole family went there for dinner after my graduation in May 1987. When I am in the Kent area, I certainly try to stop by Ray's. It always brings back great memories for me. *(Bruner, '87)*

. . . .

It was graduation night 1999 and we were at Ray's celebrating a few friends' graduation. When I went up to the bar to buy a round of drinks, the bartender said, "No charge. All drinks are on Drew Carey's tab." I thought that was the coolest thing, that Drew Carey picked up the entire bar tab for every patron of Ray's that graduation night. *(Ross, 2000)*

The Budweiser Clydesdales in front of Ray's Place. One of the many special events that has occurred at Ray's over the years. Photo courtesy of Charlie Thomas.

It is interesting that Drew Carey would do that considering he never graduated from Kent State. Carey once signed a Ray's Place menu indicating that he actually flunked out of KSU on two occasions.

• •

I'm 23 years old, and I think I have as many memories of Ray's Place as my parents, who met each other there 30 years ago. I can remember as young as three years old being carried around the bar on Watson's hip while my dad managed the downstairs bar. [Pat Watson is a longtime manager at Ray's.] I sat on the bar top eating the cheesy puffs they sold.

Fast-forward 14 years to my senior year winter formal. We were the only group of kids who went to Ray's before the dance. Played pool in our suits and dresses.

Fast-forward again three years. I'm 21. Every bartender knows my name, and I wouldn't feel safer anywhere else. I've grown up at Ray's, grown up with Charlie's son, Cameron. I consider Ray's part of my family. Wouldn't have it any other way. *(C. Stritch, '11)*

The Music Scene

A lot of good music has come out of KSU and Kent over the years. Popular bands such as Devo, 15-60-75 The Numbers Band, and the TwistOffs call Kent home. And, Chrissie Hynde of the Pretenders attended KSU. During Hynde's time in Kent, she was in a local band that included Mark Mothersbaugh, later of Devo fame. Many of these musicians have frequented Ray's as performers and customers. One TwistOffs' member (Al Mothersbaugh) worked at Ray's Place for six years. The TwistOffs used a picture of one of the paintings from the restaurant on one of their first album covers. Joe Walsh, inducted to the Rock and Roll Hall of Fame in 1998 with the Eagles, was a regular at the restaurant. He originally played in Kent as a member of the James Gang. He was also in a group called Barnstorm before embarking on a solo career.

. . . .

One Ray's Place owner, Buddy LoCicero, played in a popular local band. Buddy was the drummer in a band called the Measles. At times, Joe Walsh would join in with them. *(Shaw)*

From left to right, Mary and Buddy LoCicero and Tom Shaw in the 1970s. This group brought a number of firsts to Ray's Place. Photo courtesy of Tom Shaw.

The Walking Clampetts in 1988, the unofficial house band of Mother's Junction. Photo courtesy of The Burr.

Located above Ray's Place, Mother's became a popular band bar started by Tom Shaw and the LoCiceros in the 1970s. They converted the upstairs, which had been a pool hall. Charlie Thomas kept the band bar idea alive but changed the name to Mother's Junction. Many bands and many KSU students frequented the venue for years, listening to every kind of music that could be played. One group played there so often and became so popular they were referred to as the unofficial house band for Mother's Junction. After 30 years, the rockabilly sound of the Walking Clampetts is still popular as they continue to play venues throughout the region.

4. What did S.O.B. stand for in a past sandwich menu item?

Ray's has always been supportive of the long-standing Kent State Folk Festival (in its 47th year in 2013) as well as more recent music festivals in downtown Kent celebrating Blues and Reggae music. Mother's Junction was one of the few venues in the region to feature Reggae music over 30 years ago.

Blasting the same three songs on the old jukebox every Friday and Saturday night. *(Tayek)*

It is also interesting to note the many customer stories that include popular music. Music stories from Ray's go back as far as 70 years (from the 1940s to present), and musical styles represented include big band, folk, rock, psychedelic, and heavy metal. Music is such an important part of our memories and experiences.

The phone booth, originally built in 1980 by Tom Creech and Tom McCarthy, was relocated after Mother's Junction was converted to Ray's Upstairs.

Now inactive, the phone booth was custom built in 1980 by Tom Creech and Tom McCarthy. Occasionally someone will use the booth to make a call on a cell phone. Photo by Mikala Pritts.

A Kent business institution since 1937

The Long-Gone List

A number of bars have come and gone since Ray's Place opened in Kent. The following is a sampling of the bars from the long-gone list. The majority date from the late 1960s and later:

Moon Saloon
The Stag Bar
The Deck
The Cove
Aladdin's
The Ron-de-Vou
The Stone Jug
JB's
Filthy McNasty's
The Robin Hood
The Draft Haus
Risky Business
Little Orphan
  Annie's
The Blind Owl
Pirates Alley
Walters Café
The Dome

Shark Club
The Bar Code
The Library
Fifth Quarter
Screwy Louie's
Water St. Saloon
Big Daddy's
Orville's
Crazy Horse
Wise's
Towne House
The Rathskeller
Bellies
Carpenters
The Under-
  ground
Club Chameleon
Pat's Place

BC's
Bus Stop
Y2K
Friar Tucks
Varsity
Genesis
Stuffed Mush-
  room
Palomino
Jo & Ann's
The Barn
Cheers
Professor's Pub
Haymakers
and most recently
Firehouse Bar &
  Grille

Ray's-n-Hell

One Super Bowl Sunday my college roommate and I decided to have some fun and we dug out some old clothes—he dressed up in full regalia as a cowboy with hat, sheepskin vest, kerchief, boots, etc. The idea was for him to hit on girls as an actual cowboy who just got off the range looking to go a-courting in the big city. We couldn't believe the interest he got from the bevy of KSU girls at Ray's that evening! They were intrigued to say the least . . . "Are you really a cowboy?" . . ."Why, yes ma'am, I sure am, and you sure are a sight to this ol' cowpoke's eyes!" Funny as hell—until my buddy hit on the wrong girl (bartender's girlfriend). The sight got a bit ugly from there as he told us to leave and (in the spirit of the Old West) my buddy re-fused, claiming racism declaring that he was being singled out since he was a cowboy! Needless to say the 'Niner's won in dramatic fashion over the Bengals, and we were escorted out in dramatic fashion by the Kent police! Had to lay low from Ray's that semester, but once the smoke cleared it was business as usual for us at Ray's . . . sans the cowboy act! *(Farrar, '90)*

The Ruggers was the nickname given to a rugby team in the early 1980s that came to Ray's to wind down after their games. At times the celebrations got a bit wild and a favorite activity was to select a girl in the bar and pass her over their heads throughout the bar. This would last until the owner would intervene.

| 5. Who was Gertie? |

I lived at Ray's during the '80s. I also still work here in Kent, which is weird somehow! I still remember being passed around the bar hand over hand by the rugby players while listening to the B-52's "Rock Lobster." *(Anon, '85, '92)*

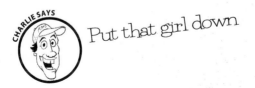

CHARLIE SAYS

Put that girl down

There's a certain table at Ray's that we call the "black hole." Every time we sit there, something out of the ordinary happens. We had just come in, and I was sitting alone saving a table for our group when a slightly deranged lady sits down across from me. She starts to quiz me and I start "goofing" on her. She starts to get louder and louder as my wife and sister-in-law come around the corner and think I've picked up a date for the night! My wife recognizes her from our high school days and starts using her real name. (She had told me a phony one.) Now she gets louder and very anxious and actually threatens to kill my wife! By this time her drunken husband, who was seated at the bar, tries to rescue her, Ray's staff arrives to escort her out. It turns out she has been bounced before and is now banned. An actual death threat at Ray's really spiced that night up! *(Duffy)*

The moose head located in the downstairs bar has become a symbol often associated with Ray's Place. Students especially have appreciated it for many years. For example, it was common practice years ago for nursing school graduates to celebrate at Ray's after they completed their nursing studies. Reliable sources report that at one point in the evening

Condom night in 1990. Even a moose likes to party at Ray's Place. Photo courtesy of the *Daily Kent Stater*.

(usually late), the celebrants would remove various undergarments and toss them on the moose antlers much to the delight of all present. No one is sure of its exact origins, but the moose head seems to have first appeared in the early 1980s and was probably part of the promotion bringing Moosehead Canadian beer to Ray's as the following story illustrates.

I have so many Ray's memories that I could share—I'm not even sure where to begin! There is one night, however, that I feel should be included above all others: the First Moosehead Night! If memory serves, it was March or April of 1980, and my friends and I had heard that Ray's was having a "Moosehead Night" to promote the introduction of Moosehead Canadian Lager into the Ray's portfolio of adult beverages. At the time many of my friends and I were living at College Towers Apartments. I shall leave the individual names of the participants out of this story, but collectively we were widely known as The Yanks!

Since it was Wednesday, which is the traditional beginning of the weekend when you're in college, we all decided to go. There were probably eight to 12 of us going, so we decided to call ahead so that Ray's would be fully prepared for our arrival. One of us dialed Ray's and warned them that the herd was on its way, which led to us all chanting in unison: "The herd is on its way! The herd is on its way! The herd is on its way!" When we arrived, the person at the door must have been clued in, because he let us all come right in as a group! He knew it was the herd, because each one of us was wearing his own pair of custom-made moose antlers! The bartenders all started yelling, "The herd is here!" This of course led to the whole bar chanting the slogan as well. (Back then, it was not uncommon for this kind of group phenomenon to occur at Ray's.)

At the bar was a man dressed in a three-piece suit, which was an unusual sight at Ray's at night. We quickly realized that he was the Moosehead rep, because rounds of Moosehead began magically appearing before us every ten minutes or so. The herd did not have to buy a beer all night! I would love to give some more details, but as the night went on, for some reason things got a little hazy. Suffice it to say that we all had a great time, and I believe that Ray's actually sold out of Moosehead that night. (*Fortlage, '85*)

. . . .

I have a lot of great memories of Ray's, but one of the best is my bachelorette party, where my friends came up with a "scavenger hunt" for me. One of the Ray's bartenders agreed to help them fulfill one by serenading me while bringing me a drink. Lots of great celebrations at Ray's for many grad school milestones! *(Taryn, '06 and '10)*

. . . .

Falling down Ray's stairs. Certainly a painless experience—until the next morning. *(Rupp)*

. . . .

I was at Ray's for the Brews-n-Blues fest. An old friend was back in Kent for a wedding and it seemed like just about everyone we knew was at Ray's. Everyone was enjoying the blues music, and then this guy and this girl get up and start dancing, which seemed pretty weird since no one else was dancing. They were really good dancers, too. The crowd enjoyed watching them dance, and then they started to grab people out to dance with them. It took a little while, but eventually they had the whole bar dancing. The band loved it! *(Anon, '12)*

. . . .

Futher Muckers—I do remember that two drinks were more than plenty. Probably why I haven't had one since the early '80s when I sprained my ankle trying to do the "Monkey Walk" with a group of friends down the middle of Franklin after partaking in a couple of Futher Muckers at Ray's. *(Anon)*

. . . .

Now when my two former roommates come to town we always go to Ray's to have a celebratory Futher Mucker! *(Bridgeman, '80)*

. . . .

I remember when my best friend told me, while we were at Ray's having lunch, she got her nipples pierced. That was a very funny conversation and one I will never forget. *(Yvette)*

6. What brand and vintage are the cash registers?

. . . .

Some friends, my husband, and I returned to Kent and Ray's after being away for many years. The bartender stopped serving one of my friends, and we were up in arms because we had never seen one person cut off in all the years we went there. We left and went to a friend's house and lo and behold, the one guy threw up all over the kitchen. Guess those Ray's bartenders know their stuff. *(Hammond)*

7. Was the upstairs phone booth ever in use at Ray's?

· ·

A group of eight and myself were all nutrition majors who would spend our Thursday evenings after a night class at Ray's with our traditional healthy Ray's staples: three baskets of Sun Stix with extra ranch dressing (sweet potatoes help prevent night blindness and the fat in ranch helps the vitamins get through) and a few pitchers of Blue Moon (the orange is a good source of vitamin C). Our professors wouldn't believe us, but the food and drink at Ray's is as nutritionally sound as the smoothies you can buy down the street. *(Gina, '07)*

· ·

In 1984 I was a sophomore at Kent and had started hanging out with some upperclassmen. One night as we were planning our evening, someone said, "Let's go to Ray's." In my innocence I said, "Where?" Of course jaws dropped and everyone looked incredulous. "What do you mean 'where'? You've never been to Ray's?" So they baptized the uninitiated in some Killian's on tap (which I love to this day). The first thing I remember was it was amazingly well lit—you could actually see the people! It was packed, wall to wall, and it was so unlike the other bars. There were students and city residents and young people and adults and faculty. It was a place where everyone felt comfortable hanging out. That was my first visit. There were many others. A few when we were politely asked to not dance on the chairs. Which we stopped immediately. *(Shantell, '84)*

· ·

Turning 21 and getting a free Futher Mucker. Writing barely legible checks for $2.91 for beers at 1:55 A.M. Carving my initials into the booths. Getting in line for the bathroom before I had to go because I would have to by the time I got to the one toilet they had. Sneaking out the back door through the kitchen to use the Loft's bathroom and then sneaking back in again. The gyro guy who parked outside. *(Anon, '85, '92)*

Ray's and Romance

> We stopped at Ray's after our wedding on the way to our reception. We surprised our wedding party and wound up getting photos taken on the bar! Those are some of our favorite photos and memories from our wedding. *(Cline-Sopko, '04, '07)*

Ray's Place holds immense meaning for many couples. Many stop by on their wedding day or share other celebrations at Ray's, while others just happened to meet the love of their life there.

SHARING A SPECIAL DAY

> After graduating from Kent State, I fell in love with the city and decided to stay—for good! Ray's grew from being a college hangout to a regular gathering place for me. So much so, in fact, I held my wedding reception upstairs at Ray's in May 1998. My friends and family still recount it as one of the best receptions they ever attended—full of great food, fun, and refrigerator magnet tossing. It was also where we gathered to say "farewell" to my husband 11½ years later when he succumbed to a brain tumor in 2009. Charlie and the wonderful staff at Ray's have treated me like family and have created a warm, welcoming establishment in which the community may celebrate all milestones (big or small) and laugh, cry, and support one another as a family. *(Yankovich, '89)*

> My wife and I were married at the Kent Newman Center on December 30, 1988. Between the wedding and the reception, our entire wedding party traveled via limo to drink a Futher Mucker and do a few shots. The groomsmen had to clear a path leading to the bar so that my bride could get in. We have wedding pictures of the bridal party with the Ray's logo in the background. Ray's was our favorite hangout and we were so happy to include it as a part of our memorable day! *(Blitz)*

(Top) The Cline-Sopko wedding party poses at Ray's Place in 2011. This wedding party is one of many that has stopped at Ray's Place over the years. Photo courtesy of Cline-Sopko.

(Bottom) The Frahlich-Diamond wedding party stopped at Ray's after their 2012 wedding. Photo courtesy of Frahlich-Diamond.

RANDOM MEETINGS

The following stories of chance meetings at Ray's Place really are true, even if they seem a bit Hollywood.

. . . .

It was the mid-80s at Ray's. The music was loud, the bar was packed, and there she was. It could have been the soft light from the old lights, or the warm glow of the wooden booth that framed her face. But I already knew I loved her. It would only take eight years to propose. Now, 20 years later, I still love her and Ray's. *(Karp, '87)*

Dan and Merri Karp randomly stopped at Ray's after a number of years of living away. It was their anniversary and they were set on a sharing a slice of their favorite peanut butter pie. It turned out to be Homecoming and the kitchen was already closed. After explaining their situation to one of the managers, they left with an entire pie!

. . . .

Wow! Do I ever remember Ray's Place. I tended bar and waited tables there from 1967 to 1969. I met my wife, class of '69, there. I served her a pizza, and the rest is history. *(Maitland, '69)*

. . . .

It was October 1977, a Wednesday night. I was in Kent visiting my girl-friend, Candy, who was attending Kent State on the five-year plan. We went to Ray's for something to eat and met some guys that we talked to the whole night. About 2 A.M., as we were leaving Ray's, we heard that Lynyrd Skynyrd's plane had crashed. That's how I remember the date. Eleven years later I married the guy I met that night, and we've been married for 23 years. *(Conrtrucci, '82)*

. . . .

My husband and I went on our first date to see *Harold and Maude* at the Filmworks at KSU. Afterwards we went to Ray's and talked for hours. I knew that night that this was the man I wanted to spend the rest of my life with. Corny but true. October 2012 was our 23rd Anniversary. *(Cobbledik, '86)*

My wife was employed by *Cleveland Magazine*, and Ray's Place was one of her customers for advertis-

ing. She called on Charlie, Creech, and/or Guido regularly. For many, many years I have been frequenting Ray's. Both my wife and I know Charlie, as well as others because of all the business and pleasure we have carried on at Ray's. One evening, we were enjoying dinner upstairs and Charlie walked by. He saw us and greeted us; "Hi, Ed . . . Hi, Rose," took a couple steps, stopped, turned, came back to our table and said, "I never put both of you together." Charlie knew us but I do not think he ever saw us together at the same time and it had finally hit him. All right, but we thought it was funny. *(Borzuk)*

I met my wife standing in line to get in to Ray's. At least that's what she said. *(Murray)*

I met a wonderful gal who eventually became my wife. I will never forget the day I first saw her at closing time. Walt Hamilton and I were cleaning the tables and putting up the chairs. In she walks—I looked at Walter and pointed to her saying, "Walt, I am going to marry that girl someday." Walt simply said, "Yeah, right, Bogart." And I said, "No, seriously!" He just chuckled. Well, sure enough—we did get married—19 years ago. *(Bogart, '86)*

I was introduced to my future wife a couple times at various Greek functions on campus. The first time I ever really talked to her was upstairs at Ray's. We were sitting at a table with some friends we had in common. I remember talking to her for about an hour and she was not particularly impressed. About half of the time she had her back turned. I do remember telling her that I was going to marry her that night. We started dating shortly thereafter and have been happily married for 14 years! *(Brewer, '96)*

I came to Kent in the fall of 1977. Ray's and Mother's quickly became a part of almost every weekend (and plenty of weekdays) for the next four years of my life! So many friends and so many good times. Many of those memories are a little foggy. But I do remember that I had a crush on Charlie Thomas. *(Holly, '81)*

. . . .

My first date with Jenn, a '68 KSU graduate, occurred at Ray's. She was 60 and I was 63. The staff is a part of our lives going on six years now. No first date discount, however. *(Baker)*

. . . .

Ray's was a place where my friends and I went to meet, catch up, and one where I got a second chance. We met up several times a month, and on one special occasion I reconnected with someone very special to me. I met Cassandra at graduation; I knew almost instantly that this woman was someone who would change my life forever. As she stood right in front of me in line, we had a conversation, getting to know each other, just passing time until it was time to step out into the real world. Cassandra was amazing, and we connected on a deep level. We began to share stories of how our closest role models, both of whom were grandparents, had passed away and how big an impact that had had on our lives. As I was getting ready to ask her for her number so that we could continue our conversation after graduation, we got split into different sides of the MAC Center.

I felt like the wind had been knocked out of me. I looked around during graduation to find her so that after I could run up real quick to congratulate her and possibly get that number. But, as fate would have it, it didn't work out as I'd hoped. Almost four months went past. Then one night, the boys and I were out at Ray's having dinner, and she reappeared. One of my friends had invited some other friends to meet up with us at Ray's. When they arrived, they came over to say hello, and there she was, right in front of me! I couldn't believe it. I sat in silence and just smiled. I looked goofy during all of this, according to my friends. Cassandra and her friends sat down at the table next to ours and ordered drinks. My friend and I went over and began talking to them, and I was able to strike up a conversation with Cassie.

I knew the moment she walked in who she was, but she had no idea who I was. We played the how-do-I-know-you game for a little bit until I asked her last name, and then it clicked for us. We talked throughout that night and several more nights at Ray's. We still come back with my friends fairly regularly. Now, Cassie and I have Ray's to thank for reuniting us and forever changing our lives for the better. Over a few drinks and the atmosphere at Ray's, we got to

9. Who was Stereo Chuck?

know each other again. Only time will tell what this second chance will give us. Thank you, Ray's, for the amazing food, service, atmosphere, and most of all giving me this second chance. *(Flounders, '11)*

. . . .

Back in the mid-80s, my friends and I enjoyed socializing at Ray's Place on the weekends. Late one Friday night with the music blasting, a couple of young ladies stood up and yelled, "Conga line!" and then formed a conga line of two and began shuffling between the tables. It wasn't long before my friends and I joined in. There must have been over two dozen people dancing the conga. What great fun it was. *(Defer, '89)*

. . . .

It was March Madness 2002 and the KSU men's basketball program had fought its way to the NCAA Elite Eight for the first time in the school's history. Ray's was the place to be, as long as you were thirsty, not claustrophobic, and not a fan of Indiana University.

I remember standing at the far end of the bar with friends and WNIR radio morning show host Stan Piatt enjoying a few pregame beverages and discovering that one of my favorite comedians (and KSU attendee) Drew Carey had made the trip home to northeast Ohio for the game. Of course he watched it at Ray's and was graciously meeting and greeting all the fired up Kentites.

A busty young woman made her way to the end of the bar and, with a sharpie marker in hand, asked if we wouldn't mind signing an autograph for her. Lacking a piece of paper, we gladly obliged putting her natural attributes to good use.

I was told by a friend that my wife came in the front door a few minutes later and asked if he had seen me inside. The exited young lady interjected, proudly showed off her fresh signatures and said, "He's with Stan at the end of the bar." Thanks, Charlie and staff! Ray's is a big reason I now call Kent home. *(Otto Orf, retired pro soccer player)*

. . . .

I met my wife of 24 years at Ray's. She left her driver's license at the bar so I had to call her. She claims it was an accident. I know better. *(Creech)*

Tom Creech has been on the staff at Ray's Place for 33 years, longer than any other employee.

Behind the Bar

EMPLOYEE MEMORIES

It's a busy Thursday lunch upstairs. Ann Marie Quitter, Tom McDonald, and I are working. Ray's is packed! Tom is taking an order from four ladies. Three order burgers, but one is unsure what she wants and is very slow in ordering. Tom is sweating, getting behind, and would like to hurry up. Finally, she places her order. The order comes, and as he is delivering the food the slow lady says, "That's not what I ordered." Her friends say, "Yes, you did!" "But I wanted all the stuff on it," she says. Tom says, "I can fix it," she is like, "No, it's okay." He says, "No, I can fix it." And they go back and forth a few times like this. We are slammed, stuff needs to be done, people are waiting. All of a sudden, Tom goes, and I quote, "Lady, just give me the f——plate." She lets go, and he runs to the back. I am bartending and start laughing my ass off. I go to the back, and Tom says, "I am soooo fired." I took over the table, and the ladies could not stop laughing. They ate and left a $20 tip with a note that said, "That was the best laugh we had in years. Thank you so much." *(D'Agati)*

Best job ever! Just want that to be known. That will probably be my favorite job working for someone else that I will ever have in this lifetime. Plus, I met my husband there. *(Weil)*

As a past employee I have many, many cherished memories, but let me just share one. I was working at the Loft making pizzas but would always go to Ray's when I got off work because Ray's was a cooler place to hang out. During the summer between my freshman and sophomore years, I worked at Cedar Point. It was during that summer that I was so determined to work at Ray's that I wrote Charlie a letter to express my desire and told him of the date and time I would be at Ray's to apply for a job. I showed up as promised and was fortunate to get a job in the kitchen cleaning dishes and cutting the fries! I was the happiest guy alive the day I started work at Ray's. I continued to work at Ray's for the remainder of my days at Kent, which afforded me the financial support I needed to finish college. I wonder if Charlie kept that letter. *(Bogart, '86)*

My first job in the hospitality business was at Ray's Place, and over the next twenty-two years of being a professional bartender and beverage consultant I have trained thousands of bartenders and servers. The first one I was responsible for teaching, though, is the one who changed my life. Sheila started at Ray's two years after I did and worked her first shift with me. I showed her around behind the bar explaining why gin was gin, showing her how to make a Futher Mucker, and impressing upon her how much studying she would need to do to pass the bartender test. She soon passed her test, scoring the first perfect score ever by a bartender at Ray's (even getting the bonus question correct), and we became friends.

Later that year at the employee Christmas party (fueled by a little bit of Jagermeister) she kissed me, and we had our first date that New Year's Eve. We've now been together for twenty years, marrying in the gazebo on Franklin Avenue, and having our reception at Ray's. I owe my career, my life, and my wife to Charlie Thomas and the Mooseheads. *(DeLuca, '94).*

. . . .

Ray's Place. Just the thought of it brings a smile to my face. So many good times and good people. My memories go back to before Charlie Thomas owned the bar. I was having lunch at Ray's with a housemate of mine, Gary Wiesband, aka Wiz, and he asked Buddy, the prior owner, for a job. Little did we know then that soon almost all of S. Depeyster Street would be working and partying at Ray's. I only worked at Ray's for a little while. The lasting memories I have and the experiences that continue today are of the friendships and the parties with the many people I have met and have worked with at Ray's. *(Cancelliere, '79, '86)*

. . . .

I started working in the kitchen, which was a lot like a Grateful Dead show. I also worked the door upstairs and downstairs, the floor, and the bar. If you told the interviewing manager all about your bartending skills, you probably didn't get the job—especially if you had worked at a stupid bar. I saw people getting hired at Ray's when they came in with no "Cocktail" baggage, had a sense of humor, and went to KSU. Had some great times with some really great people. All my closest friends came from my time

10. How many Ray's collector pint glasses are distributed during a typical Homecoming?

working at Ray's. Still go to the employee reunion party, which is really wild. You really had to do everything there to appreciate the animal that Ray's really is. *(Mothersbaugh)*

· ·

I was a proud Ray's employee for nine years! In 2003 [sic], KSU basketball had made it to the NCAA Elite Eight. It was an exciting time. I was working a dinner shift downstairs, we had the game on, and the place was packed. In walks Drew Carey (pre-"The Price Is Right"). He grabs a table in my section and tells me he would like to buy a round for the bar! He hands me his credit card, and I turn around to yell that Drew Carey wants to buy a round! He yells, "No, Lisa! Just tell people I got it when they order." Whoops! He tipped $1,000 to split up and down. Nice guy. *(Chalk)*

· ·

It was the Tuesday beer and tequila shot night (75 cents for a half pint and a shot of tequila). I was serving up the fourth or fifth round to a customer. He was feeling no pain, and I was very close to going to Pat, the manager, to talk about cutting the guy off. Then a pretty girl came up to the bar next to him to order a drink. Sloppy boy looked at her and said, "After another one of these, you can take me home if you want." He then proceeded to fall off the stool and pass out on the floor. *(Goldberg, '80)*

This line rates as one of the worst pickup lines heard by bartenders and door workers at Ray's. Joel Goldberg, who worked the door and later tended bar from 1976 through 1980, contributed this one. Joel and other Ray's employees have seen and heard just about everything you can imagine.

· ·

At one point almost the entire kitchen staff was in the same fraternity. To us the bar was called Raystaugamma. *(Anon)*

· ·

I worked at Ray's Place a little over four years. However, I didn't just "work" there, and this wasn't just a "job." Everyone there became my family. The Ray's of Our Lives was the most memorable, exciting time of my life. I grew up there, became an adult. I have a place in my heart now and forever for

Charlie, Guido, Tom, Watson, and all my wonderful friends that I made during my time at Ray's. Without the excep-

11. What is current owner Charlie Thomas's middle name?

tional life experience and support from Ray's Place, I honestly don't know where I would be today. I am blessed to have shared this experience with so many wonderful people. *(Kugelman)*

37

. . . .

I worked at Ray's in the summer of 1966. It was mainly a beer and pizza place for both "town and gown" customers. I was between a master's and a doctorate in history. One day, two KSU coaches, basketball and track, came in and sat at the bar. A minute or so later, a basketball player and his girlfriend came in and sat at one of my booths. The player said "I'll have Millers," to which I replied, "No, you won't." We went back and forth until I finally said, "Look over my shoulder at the bar." He looked and said, "You're right. I'll have an orange drink." It's so neat to hear that Ray's is still operating after 75 years. *(Eaton, '67, '73)*

. . . .

I will never forget Charlie. I have owned my own business almost since the day I graduated from KSU. I employ a great staff, over 80 people, all loyal and longtime employees. I owe everything I ever learned about being a great boss to Charlie. Aside from his employees being loyal to him, he certainly returns the favor. It's amazing that I graduated over 17 years ago, and he always remembers me and my wife every time we see him. This loyalty resonates through his entire staff and his managers. Every time I meet someone who went to Kent State, I am proud to tell them that I worked at Ray's Place! "You can get a cheeseburger at Ray's, but you can't get a beer at McDonald's." I think that's how it went. *(Morris, '95)*

. . . .

I worked as waiter at Ray's for two years back in 1958 and 1959. It was a wonderful experience, with most of our customers being military veterans. Rocky and Andy Flogge were great people to work for. During my career after graduating from KSU, I worked for many managers, but no one was a better manager than these two. Rocky had a great way of letting you know that you were doing something wrong without you immediately even knowing that you were being corrected, like the time I learned how to carry six cups of coffee in one hand. In retrospect, I can't believe I was so stupid to take such a risk. *(Scheidler, '60)*

38

· ·

At the beginning of my senior year, I decided to run for senior class president, even though I had never run for office previously, nor did I even serve on a class committee. Of course, through working at Ray's I met a lot of students. Many of these students turned out to vote, including many veterans and other students who never voted in a class election before, and I won the election. I could not have done it without my friends at Ray's.

The class of 1960 was the semi-centennial year for KSU. As senior class president, I participated in many ceremonial functions the university had to celebrate its 50 years. Giving a speech at our class commencement was a special role I had as class president. Having senior class president on my resume was very helpful in getting a job with the top CPA firm upon graduation. I feel that my short employment at Ray's was a long-term career-changing event. I have wonderful memories of Ray's and my senior year. This all started with my working at Ray's. *(Scheidler, '60)*

Vanetta "Gertie" Gritton, right front, and fellow employees ca. 1960. Gertie was a fixture at Ray's for 40 years. Photo courtesy of Charlie Thomas.

I worked at Ray's Place for five years. The first of many memories was getting hired. I was flat broke and in desperate need of a job. So broke, my phone had been turned off. I remember having less than $10 in the bank the day Tom Creech called my boyfriend, asked for me, and said, "Hey, your mom says you really need a job." I said, "Wow, you know my mom?" and he said, while laughing, "No, silly, I called her because she is your emergency contact. Come in for an interview in an hour."

I was so happy. Who would take that extra step? I know they had a stack of applications, they always do. I took the job, even though I had to drop a class and work the door during the coldest months ever in Ohio's history. Seriously! The Grateful Dead had to cancel their show in March 1992, an inside show, because of the cold! Anyway, I really appreciated and loved Tom, Charlie, and the rest of the wonderful crew I was privileged to work with, party with, and call my friends. Still do. *(Burkland)*

I had the luck of dating not one, but two fabulous Ray's employees, Sparky Atzberger and John Bando. At the time, I got to understand the rare privilege of the coveted post of working at Ray's Place for Charlie Thomas and of being the lady on that employee's arm. Having been a server-bartender at other establishments for over 20 years, I find the trust, appreciation, and warmth Charlie paid to his employees nothing short of amazing. "Nailing it," as they used to call it, was a wonderful policy where broke employees could eat and drink and have the cost subtracted from their next paycheck. I know both boyfriends took advantage of this many times.

I have been a fixture at the annual Ray's party for more than 15 years and have watched the many faces and events that are always surprising, wonderfully creative, and just pure CRAZY. Sentimentally teary-eyed, I corner Charlie at each party, telling him just how wonderful, generous, and spirited he is for providing so many memories.

Inadvertently, I married Ray's employee John Bando, and we now have three kids who frequent Ray's whenever we are in Kent. One day our kids may go to school at KSU and have the privilege of working and playing at Ray's, where the memories will only get richer for our family. *(Bando, '89)*

I was bartending one night when a student named Mark was sitting at the bar close to the center. He was drinking for a while and was slurring his words but was still pretty talkative. All of a sudden, I noticed that he had a lit bar candle in his hand and started to put it up to his lips to take a drink. Crazy! I stopped him from drinking the candle but will never forget the memory. *(Wiz)*

I worked at Ray's from 1991 through 1997 and have thousands of stories that should not be published. What I can tell or try and explain is the way Ray's and Mother's used to be, or at least how I remember them. The atmosphere was simply old school Rowdy. People came out to Ray's to get hammered and get loud. Every night was a good night at Ray's, even on slow nights, because the local bartenders would migrate over, and the bar would go nuts after midnight. Tuesday night would kick off the "weekend" with toy night; Wednesday night was always staffed with the best-looking bartenders; Thursday through Saturday were just nuts. Every week was the same thing: there would be a line out the door to the alley by 10 P.M., going one for one at the door, busy till last call inside. At last call, we always counted down and all yelled, "Laaaaaaast Caaaaaaaallllllll," while ringing the cowbell. Most times the crowd yelled, too. I have even more stories of employee events from our annual Christmas party, Brown's bus trip, and the coveted Spring Party, but they cannot be published. *(Levicki, '96)*

12. What brand of television was the first one at Ray's in 1946?

When Buddy and Mary and Tom and Jay bought Ray's Place in 1975, I initially bemoaned the idea of someone else running it. But they sensed that Ray's could appeal to both the town folk and the students. The menu and the beer list expanded and the need for interior signage became obvious. Buddy, having seen my signs for the poetry readings, hired me to do signs for specials and special events in the bar. Ray's was popular with everyone and brought new life to that part of downtown Kent. I was never much into the North Water Street scene, other than going to listen to music occasionally. I still preferred the family friendly atmosphere of Ray's. I hesitate to say wholesome, but compared to North Water Street, well . . . yes, Ray's was actually wholesome. Ray's was a neighborhood bar, with an increasing number of students discovering it. *(Muenzenmayer, '72).*

Buddy, Mary, and Tom started one of the first band bars in the area called Mother's. Charlie Thomas later renamed it Mother's Junction.

· ·

I worked for my brothers, Rock and Andy, as a waiter at Ray's for a number of years. My brother Rock told me that Lou Holtz actually proposed to his wife at Ray's. *(Flogge, '59)*

Al Flogge, youngest of the nine Flogge siblings, worked at Ray's in the late 1950s. His Ray's and KSU education carried him far into a successful career in the corporate world. He collected many photographs and letters from performing artists such as Elvis Presley and others. He donated the A. J. Flogge Performing Arts Collection of memorabilia to the Kent State University Libraries' Special Collections and Archives. Al was recognized as the KSU Distinguished Alumnus and Homecoming Parade Marshal for 1983. He is in the Flogge family photograph on page 59. Included in the photograph is the refrigerator he purchased for his family at age nine. Since Charlie Thomas was selected as Grand Marshal for the 2013 KSU Homecoming parade, that gives Ray's Place two Grand Marshals . . . 30 years apart. A rare distinction indeed!

LIFE AT THE DOOR

Ray's Place is unique in that all employees start out working the door. It can be a pretty tough assignment and the experiences can be wild. A few sample stories illustrate that working the door at a college bar has its moments.

· ·

My memories of Ray's Place go back to the days when Charlie first bought the bar. When Charlie bought Ray's, there was a violation on the liquor license for serving a minor. When you buy the liquor license, you get any violations with it, and this violation came from the prior owner. Charlie put doormen in place to check IDs, and I was one of the first doormen. As you can imagine, we were not very popular to the patrons who were used to just walking in, especially the underage ones.

Back in the late '70s, we had 3.2 percent beer for 18- to 21-year-olds, so we used a black [hand] stamp for "high" and a red one for "low." People were always devising ways to remove the red stamp and create a black one.

Life at the door could get hectic as you saw a fair number of fake IDs. Also patrons were always trying to take a little piece of Ray's home with them—beer mugs, shot glasses, even beer pitchers. One time a police officer brought me back some of the Ray's glassware that he confiscated out on the street. Sometimes the work was dangerous, and one of my fellow door-men got a beer bottle broken over his hand. While I was never physically assaulted, I did hear plenty of verbal abuse. Like I said, when the doormen first started, we were not real popular.

One thing about Ray's, though, was that the fellow employees always had your back and still do to this very day, 30 plus years later. One night the bar was overfilled with partiers as was usually the case, and a person I knew from class thought he would bypass the line and walk right past me into the bar. I went in after him, and by the time I had him pulled back out the door, Donnie and three other bartenders where right there to help me. I have been fortunate to share a lot of good times with my fellow Ray's employees. So thanks Charlie for the job back then when I was a poor college student and thanks for over 30 years of friendship and good times. (Cancelliere, '79 and '84)

· ·

Back when I was carding at the door, a guy my age walked out and handed me a $5 bill with his full name and number on it. I asked him why he wrote it on cash rather than just a piece of paper and he told me, "I wanted to make sure you would hold onto it," as he winked and walked out. I came home that night to my roommate and told her the story. Turned out she knew the guy—and his girlfriend. So that next day when I went for groceries, I made sure I paid using that bill—without crossing out his name and number. (Spiroff)

13. Which Ray's employee has the longest tenure?

· ·

If you have bartended at Ray's you have also most likely spent considerable time at the door checking IDs. Catching fakes demands skill, concentration, experience, and sometimes just a non-English mother tongue. One busy night a girl handed me an ID that I immediately recognized as a Swedish bus pass since I'm from Sweden. "Time for some fun," I thought. I asked the girl where she was from. She answered Sweden, adding that she had given me a Swedish ID. I proceeded to ask if she then also spoke Swedish. "Yes," she said, upon which I then asked her, in Swedish, if she understood what I was saying since I was now addressing her in her supposed native language. She looked, literally, dumbfounded and did not have much to say. I said I was going to keep her "ID" since it was a badly laminated bus pass from Stockholm, and not an ID. She turned away and sulked off, in seeming disbelief over her bad luck. *(Skold, '93)*

Thomas Skold sent this story while traveling by train in Sweden. He was with his brother Henrick who also worked at Ray's and still lives in Kent.

· ·

Working the door is the most important and the suckiest job in the place. I worked the door at Mother's Junction for a few years. At first I hated catching people with fake IDs, but after a while it got be sort of a badge of honor. We would actually keep track of the number we got each night. One guy actually caught 30 in one night. That must have been a record. *(Mothersbaugh)*

When asked how she liked working the door after her first 20 minutes, a new employee commented, "I feel like I'm working in a fishbowl!"

THE MANAGER'S VIEW

The Ray's Place management team is a unique group of employees. Most of them have worked at Ray's Place for more than 25 years. They have seen and heard just about anything and everything employees in a college-town bar can experience. They are fiercely loyal to owner Charlie Thomas and, like Charlie, they genuinely enjoy what they do. It's common to see them shaking hands with or embracing customers. They also like to keep themselves entertained, which often shows up in the way they deal with customers. They can do some first-rate wisecracking, which is evident in the following memories shared from their view as managers.

· ·

I walked into the bar one night and here's this guy hammering nails into one of the tables. *(Creech)*

The Ray's Place management team in 2012 has an average tenure of 25 years. Photo courtesy of Charlie Thomas.

· ·

We have our own Ray's vibe . . . we like being unique . . . no need to be corporate. *(Cowles)*

· ·

A customer who has been away for a while might hear, "Haven't seen you in a while . . . where ya been . . . prison? . . . . the seminary?" *(Melin)*

Ray's Place is known for having a wide assortment of international beers. The following exchange was heard one evening at Ray's. Customer says to a bartender, "I see you have quite a few beers." Reply: "Yes, we do." "Do you have any light beers?" "Yes, we have a couple. We also have root beer."

· ·

One group of customers never seemed to mind us serving them bourbon in an ashtray, and the Ruggers liked drinking beer from a work boot. *(Creech)*

Many families were started here. *(Stritch)*

Toilet replacement became an art at Ray's Place. Managers have replaced so many broken toilets over the years they could do one in about 20 minutes.

・・ **45**
We actually kept a backup supply of toilets since they were broken so often. *(Nave)*

This is less of a problem now as customers have calmed down some, including students. Managers view Ohio's legal drinking age being raised to 21 in 1987 as helping to improve overall rowdy behavior. However, the drinking age was still 18 when the following event occurred.

・・
It was the early '80s, and Tom Madar was working the door and Pat Stritch the floor. An argument erupted between two guys. Pat went over to calm things down and proceeded to get sucker-punched in the process. I yelled out the door to Tom and managed to grab the guy who had hit Pat as he was heading for the door. Long hair was still popular then, so I pulled out a big handful of the guy's hair as he got shoved out the door. Pat was glad to see the guy's hair and to know he didn't get away without some degree of pain. Even after all this, the guy kept trying to get back in the bar. I think he wound up in jail that night. *(Zoller)*

Vendor Memories

I have been a food representative to Ray's Place since 1993. It has been a pleasure working with the different chefs over the years. I am very fortunate to have partnered most recently with Chef Bob Paone. Bob has carried on the traditional dishes adding fresh variety and trends to the menu. On behalf of U.S. Foods, I thank Ray's for the business and look forward to many more years of servicing Ray's Place. *(Ulreich)*

I was so thankful that through all the changes over the years, Ray's was still the neighborhood bar and restaurant that the whole family could enjoy. It's been a few years since I've been back to northeast Ohio, but when I do get back I'll surely call up some friends and say, "See you at Ray's." *(Muenzenmayer, '72)*

Kenny Muenzenmayer did artwork for Ray's Place for almost 20 years. He created interior promotional posters for Toy Night, Spaghetti Night, and others. He also did special artwork for employee parties and functions. Much of his artwork is still on the walls. He also painted the murals seen in the bar capturing some of the more iconic images of the early Ray's Place. Kenny worked for and personally knew three of the four owners of Ray's.

I had the pleasure of working with the Flogge brothers as their food vendor for many years. I started calling on them at Ray's in 1952 after I got back from Korea. In addition to our fine business relationship, we became great friends. I also got to know almost all their family members. Andy and I did a lot of fishing together at lakes all over the area as well as in Canada. Rocky was the guy who seemed to be able get tickets for any event, especially sporting. He did a lot of favors for a lot of people, including me. He helped my wife and me get our wedding rings. They were wonderful guys from a wonderful family, and it was an honor to do business with them. *(Matheos)*

Are We Making This Up?

SOME UNIQUE CUSTOMER MEMORIES

> I was 18 years old and drafted in July 1943. We were waiting for the train to take us to Fort Hayes Army Camp in Columbus, Ohio. The train was late, and we were hot, standing in the sun. Three of us sneaked over to Ray's Place for a last beer in Kent.
>
> I came home three years later, and went to Ray's to celebrate, and still go back once in a while in the hot summer to sit next to the brick wall and cool off. *(Shircliff)*

Joseph A. Shircliff was 87 years young when he contributed this memory and has the distinction of contributing the oldest story in this book. He has been a Ray's Place customer through all four owners. Joe celebrated 70 years at Ray's Place in 2013. Joe and his wife, Peg, raised six children in Suffield, Ohio. He worked driving a truck at Goodyear for 43 years. Joe likes to spend time with his wife, children, grandchildren, and friends. He also collects bottle openers and shot glasses numbering in the hundreds.

With the shot wheel in the background, WWII veteran Joe Shircliff enjoys a beverage at Ray's as he has done through all four owners. Photo by Mikala Pritts.

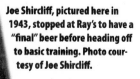

Joe Shircliff, pictured here in 1943, stopped at Ray's to have a "final" beer before heading off to basic training. Photo courtesy of Joe Shircliff.

· ·

Going for lunch at Ray's with a group of friends, and leaving at 2 A.M.!
(Cobbledick)

· ·

Rocky Flogge was the bartender I remember most. He was more than a
friend to many of his GI customers. Some worked part time to pay for their
meals. When the $20 checks came, some men just signed it over to Rocky
as he often ran a tab so they could eat. *(Andreas, '54)*

· ·

I started at KSU in September 1957 after serving in the U.S. Army for three
years. During my first quarter I met a number of other veterans who were
members of a local fraternity called the "Collegiates." Their hangout was
Ray's Place, which we also called "Rocky's," as the owner at that time was
Rocky Flogge. Rocky eventually became an honorary member of our fraternity. We would gather at the fraternity house at 132 South Lincoln Street to
watch the Browns games, and Rocky would come over with a keg and food
and spend the day.

    A number of the members (Sam Morris and John Tarr, for example)
worked at Ray's, and we hung out there daily. My favorite meal was the
pork chops. Rocky helped me get a job at the Kent Liquor Store just before
I married my wife, Carol, in 1959. My first big mistake after we were married was when Carol made pork chops one day and I announced they were
pretty good but not as good as Ray's Place! It was a long time before she
made pork chops again!

    My daughter, Sherri Bevan Walsh, the current Summit County pros-
ecutor, was born in Kent in 1960, and the first bar we took her to was, of
course, Ray's Place. My wife and I try to get to Kent at least once a year and
the only place we stop to eat is Ray's. When I organized a reunion in 2010 of
the Collegiates Alumni, the large attendance, I believe, was due to the fact
we initially met at Ray's Place. *(Bevan, '61)*

· ·

14. Guido is a nickname for what Ray's manager?

For all the amazingly good times we've had at
Ray's, a few sad moments flood our memories,
too. We've lost dear friends and family to ill-
nesses, but during their battles they still made the trip to Ray's. We even made
special arrangements to get a wheelchair in the front door to have our gang
together for what we thought might be that last time . . . and it was. *(Duffy, '74)*

Sometimes the place is so crowded (Homecoming and St. Patrick's Day come to mind) that the servers can't get from the kitchen window to the tables so they have to close the kitchen. A restaurant that's too busy to serve food! At least they can still serve drinks. *(Anon)*

My senior year of college housing decision was based on the location of Ray's. I lived on the corner of Franklin Avenue and Williams Street. Every Thursday afternoon after class I would stop in for a Foster's draft and a Mama Mushia. Later we'd sing to "Brown-Eyed Girl" on the jukebox and eat two pickled eggs from the big jar on the counter by the moose. *(Matticola, '92)*

My best memories from college come from Ray's Place. Ray's was always the late-night place where we all met up to end the night. My friends and I would edge our way to the front of the line to get in and go straight up-stairs to dance and mess with others. Shared a lot of fond memories with friends there that I will never, ever forget. From my 21st birthday, to late nights, to happy hours, to grad classes being held there, to meeting years later for alumni events, Ray's Place will always hold a special place in my heart. *(Miller, '06, '08)*

Every time I was leaving Kent at the end of the semester or coming back, my friends and I had to eat at Ray's. From my farewell dinner before I left for Italy to leaving for the summer, and every time I visit Kent, I have to eat and drink at Ray's! It's where I brought my parents and grandparents every time they came to visit! Ray's holds a lot of my college memories and will hold many memories to come. *(Oprean, '11)*

I have very fond memories of Ray's Place during my time at KSU. At the time, I felt a little uneasy with the thought of eating all my meals at one of the many restaurants and diners in Kent. But I soon found Ray's, and it was as comfortable as being at home. The owners made everyone feel wel-come, and the food was great, plentiful and affordable. And the beer was pretty good, too. To this day, I can still see Rocky dressed in his customary white apron mingling with students and flashing his ever-present smile. It was the place to go, to meet friends, to seek sympathy when things went awry, to celebrate when things went well or just hang out. The last time I was in Kent, I dropped in and the faces had changed, but not the surroundings or the memories. *(Jenkins, '59)*

· ·

My first memory of Ray's Place is the spaghetti dinner special, which I believe was either $1 or $1.10. It included salad, bread, and meatballs and was a good, cheap meal for a hungry student. It also allowed a "big spender" to take a date to dinner. Next comes the jukebox, which we played continuously, especially Ella Fitzgerald's "Mr. Paganini" and the Trio's "Where Have All the Flowers Gone?" From 1958 to 1962, Ray's was my hangout and the official bar of my fraternity, Kappa Sigma. However, we always called it Rocky's because of the co-owner back then, who always seemed to be behind the bar no matter when we went there. His brother was always in the kitchen. *(Flanagan, '62)*

Verna Flogge is credited with preparing the first pizza available in a Portage County restaurant. It was also available for carryout, which was a novel idea at the time.

The all-you-can-eat spaghetti feast on Wednesday nights also became a popular tradition at Ray's and still continues. The advertisement for it featured people eating spaghetti off a man. (See page 81.)

· ·

16. Buddy LoCicero, a Ray's Place owner in the 1970s, was in a band called the Measles. What instrument did he play?

My fondest memory goes back to the days when Andy Flogge ran the bar and my father and I would walk downtown to watch the trains coming in, cast a few rocks into the Cuyahoga River, and head over to Ray's Place. In those days the walls were hung with fish trophies and an autographed photo of KSU alumnus and Major League shortstop Gene Michael. Dad would have a beer with his friends from the Jaycees while I sat on a stool, fully content with a stack of dimes to play the bowling machine, with a shaker of stuff perched on the rail that helped the heavy metal disc glide under the pins and back to my hand. I've had my share of beer there myself in the decades since, but that's the memory I cherish the most. *(DuBois)*

What memories do I not have of Ray's? From the awkwardly intimate moments of two inebriated college students groping one another at the bar to having a few too many myself, each time I go to Ray's I expect a new story to unfold. One particular occasion, however, stands out from the rest. Everyone who ventures to Ray's on their 21st or even their 52nd birthday knows that the infamous drink wheel always seems like a plausible option, if only for reasons of forgetting the very age one goes out to celebrate.

On my particular occasion, just some three years ago, I decided to spin the wheel and hope for the best—Jack Daniel's, Jim Beam, Knob Creek, or even Old Crow, just to keep it classy. Much to my dismay, and the delight of a couple of my friends and the borderline sadistic bartender, the wheel landed on Jagermeister. Unfortunately, the Jager itself went down a bit heavy, chased with a few sips of whatever random IPA aforementioned bartender slid my way that particular evening, most likely to the tune of Bell's Two Hearted Ale. *(Harley, '99)*

• •

Ah . . . Ray's . . . I can still remember sneaking in when I was in high school in the late '60s and then going upstairs to shoot pool and gamble with my buds . . . yes, it was a pool hall back then . . . boy, those were the days . . . and Charlie Thomas, he was a bartender at the Loft . . . great guy . . . in fact, I bought my first stereo from him . . . a Kenwood, I think . . . he sold the stuff out of his apartment at Silver Meadows . . . you knew he was going to make it someday . . . Ray's was a great place back then and still is! *(Simmons)*

Charlie Thomas did business at this time under the name Stereo Chuck.

• •

My favorite Ray's memory was grabbing dinner and drinks with my friends every Thursday night my senior year of college. We dubbed ourselves "The Ray's Gang," and we sat at the same table every week. Our trusty waitress Jessica was there to greet us every week with our favorite beers in hand. In time she learned all our names, our favorite beers, and even what we majored in. Jess became an honorary member of the gang and every week felt like we had walked onto the set of "Cheers," where everybody knew our names. Ray's is, and always will be, the bar of choice for The Ray's Gang. *(Tilson, '10)*

. . . .

Ray's Place to me is more than just a bar; it's a family restaurant. My family knows that it's one of my favorite places to eat. Once you've had French onion soup there you don't want it anywhere else. I've been there on plenty of occasions, for birthdays, with friends, on dates, and with family. Every time I open those doors, the first thing I remember is when my dad and I would sit at the bar eating hamburgers, and that's one thing that'll stay with me for years to come. *(Kailawyn)*

. . . .

Every time I go home and need a ride back to KSU, my father always is more than willing. It goes unsaid that when we arrive in Kent, we are going to Ray's for a beer and a burger. It has become a tradition in my family. Any time my dad talks with his friends or family members about Kent, Ohio, or my schooling at Kent State he asks, "You boys ever heard of Ray's?" Then he goes on to rave about how great the burgers are, and how the only beer you should buy in that place is the Dortmunder Gold.

Ray's Place is not the reason I went to Kent State, but I know for a fact it is the reason why my father loves coming to visit. It is also a small incentive for him to keep paying my tuition. I know for a fact that I'll be coming back after I graduate; and I know where I will be eating: Ray's Place. *(Corcoran, '13)*

Entertainer Drew Carey, fourth from left, with the Ray's Place staff in 2002. Ray's employees meet some interesting customers. Photo courtesy of Charlie Thomas.

· ·

I first heard about Ray's Place from my dad, who was a member of the Delta Upsilon fraternity at Kent State during the 1950s. He was a Ray's regular when it was popularly known as a frat bar and fondly recalls slipping into Ray's for a quick lunch and beer between classes and hanging out with his fraternity brothers on weeknights. *(Pate, '88)*

· ·

I discovered Ray's allure when I attended Kent State in the 1980s, and I often took my dad there for burgers and beer when he came to visit or take me home for the weekend. We sat in the very same wooden booths he had sat in 30 years earlier as we shared memories, old and new, over frosty mugs of Killian's (with lemon, of course).

Ray's was always hopping at night, especially Thursday through Saturday nights, but I enjoyed lazy summer afternoons at Ray's when my friends and I would walk there from our Glen Morris apartments and enjoy Gertie's chili, baskets of fries, and Calistoga sodas (Black Currant was my favorite). I can still picture the jukebox in the corner that somehow always played Blondie's "One Way or Another," the gigantic jar of pickles on the bar, the glass cooler that chilled exotic import beers that I couldn't afford, the little window peeking into the kitchen, the friendly bartenders, the standing room only, and the charged atmosphere that screamed "This is the place to be." *(Pate, '88)*

· ·

During my first semester as a freshman at KSU, my parents received my interim grade report in the mail. I was earning a "Z" in my Freshmen Orientation class, which meant I was failing a pass/fail course. I should never have scheduled a 7:45 A.M. class on a Friday. My dad drove from Youngstown that night and took me to Ray's where he ordered a Munster Burger (remember those?) and I a Mo-Fo. He proceeded to read me the riot act on behalf of my mother and himself and to commandeer my checkbook. I can remember the exact booth in which we sat (the one under the stairs next to the jukebox). I was given an ultimatum: shape up or ship out. That moment could've led to the end of my educational career, but it allowed me to look at what I was doing and make adjustments. For me, going to KSU represented freedom, enlightenment, and opportunity. I am glad I can still go back to the place where I realized I needed to get my act together and throw one back with my dad. These days I cover the tab when he lets me. *(Kaschak, '95 and '02)*

Ray's was "my place" from 1978 to 1982. Going there felt like an episode of "Cheers"—everyone knew your name, and we were all there for fun and stress relief. I remember breaking the record on the Pac-Man game in 1980—I felt like a rock star! Ray's is central to my Kent memories and I still visit when I'm in the area. *(Varian)*

I grew up in Kent and have lived here my entire life. Ray's has been such a big part of my life that I incorporated a part of it into my home. To me the one piece in Ray's that stands out is the moose head above the bar. Because of this, I purchased a moose head similar to the one at Ray's, and it now hangs majestically above one of my fireplaces. *(Pfeiffer, '94 and '04)*

When I come back to Kent, I'll usually just head downtown on Saturday for beer at Ray's Place. *(Anderson, '94)*

Major Craig Anderson is the copilot of Marine One, the United States Marine Corps helicopter for President Obama.

The original Ray's Place bar ca. 1940. Photo courtesy of Charlie Thomas.

A Town-Gown Institution

The relationship between a university and the town where it is located is often a unique one. The town-gown dynamics are sometimes a function of the relative sizes of the university and the town. In the case of the city of Kent and Kent State University, the relationship is essentially a large university in a small city. As such, the university is a major contributor to many aspects of city life. For example, the local economy is heavily affected by the university. The university is by far the largest employer in the city, and many of the cultural, entertainment, and sporting events are connected to the university. Many residents live and work in the city, while others commute yet often shop and dine there. Thousands of students who occupy off-campus housing also shop, dine, and party in Kent. The "gown" aspect has a positive impact on the overall economic well-being of the city and on the quality of life. Student groups such as fraternities and sororities, for example, frequently volunteer in the local public schools, host food drives for the county's needy, and engage in other community service projects.

A trade-off to the many benefits of having a large university in a small city is that the students can sometimes annoy the local citizens. Kent, like other cities with a large university, has to deal with block parties and unruly students. This can cause friction in the town-gown relationship and strain community services, which the townspeople pay for with local taxes. Ray's Place has contributed many positive aspects to the town-gown relationship in Kent. KSU and the City of Kent were recognized by the International Town-Gown Association in April 2013 for outstanding cooperation.

· ·

I remember walking in and taking a seat in the first booth on the right in a dark corner with the stairs angling up over our heads. A friendly smiling over-size cherub of a man greeted my friend and welcomed me as he took our order, which was a large order of spaghetti that my friend suggested. He made his way back to the kitchen all the while smiling, talking, and laughing with the other patrons of the bar. This, of course, was Rocky.

From our spot in the corner I could see all that was going on. The families eating dinner, some college students, and the regulars at the bar talking with a tall affable man with a somewhat shy demeanor and a reassuring smile. Kind of like a favorite uncle. This was Andy. *(Muenzenmayer, '72)*

Walter Ink ran a barbershop in Kent for many years. Former KSU presidents Bowman and Schwartz were regular customers at Ink's, as were Rocky and Andy Flogge. Walt has been a regular Ray's customer since 1952. He was active in local politics, serving on city council a number of times. Some of his informal council meetings were conducted at Ray's Place.

• •

Aside from my actual reason to come to KSU, the next best experience I had was the vast amount of time I spent with my collegiate brothers, relishing the food and drink at Ray's Place. In fact, our independent fraternity had its beginning in Ray's Place. Memories of Andy and Rocky will live with me for whatever years I have remaining. They were two great guys who always had time to share with us. Indeed, KSU and Ray's Place are two ideal institutions that definitely shaped my future. *(Bakalar, '61)*

• •

When I think of Kent, I think of Ray's Place. My friends and I would go to Ray's about five nights a week. A typical great time included chatting with the friendly bartenders, drinking Killian's Red drafts, singing along with all the great music on the jukebox ("These Boots Were Made For Walking" was a favorite), meeting new friends, and trying to find a ride home. I could never say no to going to Ray's—I'd be afraid of missing out on a great time! *(Baker, '91)*

• •

I am what you would call a legacy member of both Kent State University and Ray's Place. My father graduated from KSU in 1981 and Ray's was his bar of choice. All the bartenders knew his name, and he had a special booth that was his and his alone (the third booth on the right when you walk in the front door; you know which one I'm talking about). I remember we would take a field trip to Kent at least once a year where we would walk around campus and I would get the Mark Tilson tour. He would show me the dorms he lived in, the buildings he had class in, and the house where he partied at and saw Arsenio Hall do stand-up. The tour always concluded with a trip to Ray's, where we both would treat ourselves to their world-famous cheeseburgers and Sun Stix. When I chose to go to Kent State for college, I also chose Ray's as my bar of choice. I felt honored and proud to carry on the tradition and legacy my dad started all those years ago both at Kent and at Ray's. *(Tilson, '10)*

17. Who painted the downstairs murals?

. . . .

Ray's was not just a bar. It was an inspiration. You hadn't truly experienced all of Kent State until you could say you were old enough (or smart enough) to get into Ray's. Ray's was the central point of all things Kent State. It wasn't a meeting place, it was the meeting place; it was the destination. The food, the beer selection, the atmosphere, the memories. Ray's was and always will be what I remember most about Kent State. *(Westergren, '93)*

. . . .

My wife and I went to Ray's Place when we were first married in 1954. Later we took our kids there, too. The T-bone steak was my favorite. It was $1.25. Andy always spoiled the kids. He and Rocky were very generous people, especially to veterans and college students. Rocky even helped me buy my wife's engagement ring. Very unusual for someone to help people out like that. I also loved Gertie's chili. I remember when Tom, Buddy, and Mary took over and brought new beers to the place. And Charlie Thomas still knows what I like to eat and drink when I go to Ray's. *(Ink)*

. . . .

My maternal grandmother was in the first graduating class of the Kent State Normal College, which later became KSU. Her daughter (my mom), her granddaughter (my sister), and her great granddaughter (my niece), also graduated from KSU, making our family the only four-generation direct-line family of KSU graduates. (Not to mention the cousins, aunts, uncle, and me, all of whom graduated from KSU.) The aforementioned does not even include anyone from my father's side of the family.

In a nutshell, I lived in Kent and literally had more than 100 relatives in town. Every time I walked home from school (or anywhere else) and decided to do something stupid, I was met at the front door with a spanking. I never could figure out how mom knew and who that damn bird was that told her what I did. I finally learned that just because I don't know a cousin, doesn't mean they don't know me. I later became a cop in Kent, which somehow seemed ironic.

I went to Ray's as a child with both grandfathers. I went to Ray's with my dad. I went to Ray's as a young man with friends. I went to Ray's with my children, and I've been to Ray's (best of all) with my grandson. *(Hostler, '99)*

Many, many students worked at Ray's over the years. In fact, the current owner, Charlie Thomas, has employed 857 KSU students since he bought Ray's Place in 1978. That's an average of about 30 students each year and represents almost 100 percent of his employees. All of his management team attended and/or graduated from KSU. Charlie is also a graduate of the KSU business school, as is his wife, Diane. One employee, Tom Creech, has been working there since 1979, a year after Charlie Thomas took ownership.

In addition to attracting college professors and students, Ray's has always had a following of Kent citizens not associated with the university.

Ray's has been an active supporter of KSU athletics for almost 70 years. Ray's Place is an active advertiser in game programs and supporter of promotional events for the athletic department. Many KSU athletes over the years have eaten at Ray's Place; some have worked there, too. KSU coaches used to show game films there.

• •

Charlie gives his time and money to make this a better town, and he does not expect anything in return. That is why, as a small token of my appreciation, I play my bagpipes at Ray's on St. Patrick's Day. If bagpipes make people come into Ray's or stay longer and spend, I'll play for Charlie. Charlie has developed a feeling of comfort in downtown Kent that has resulted in people from all around the area coming in and visiting other businesses, thus creating jobs and opportunities for other businesses in town.

Charlie has perfected the "nod bar." A nod bar is the place that has so many regular customers, from such a large area, that people see each other on the street and nod at each other because they feel a connection from seeing each other at Ray's. In other words, if you're a friend of Ray's Place, you're a friend of mine. *(Hostler, '99)*

The current ceiling light fixtures downstairs at Ray's Place are the original ones from 1937.

A group of friends, including "Harry the Jeweler," at Ray's (year unknown). For years these regular customers let themselves in each morning through the back entrance of Ray's and made their own coffee before the owners arrived. Photo courtesy of Charlie Thomas.

The Flogge family at Ray's Place in 2012. Standing left to right: Maryanna and Henry Dannemiller, Frank Coz Jr., and Joe Flogge. *Seated:* Charles Flogge. Joe owns a golf course in the area, continuing the Flogge tradition in sports. Frank's son, Frank Coz III, is a student at KSU and worked at Ray's Place, where Flogge family members have worked since 1946. Photo courtesy of Mikala Pritts.

Most of the Flogge family worked at Ray's at one time or another, and most family functions were held there, including this photo of Mary and Joe Flogge, seated, and their family on their 40th wedding anniversary in 1954. Photo courtesy of Al Flogge.

Verna Flogge, wife of Andy. Photo courtesy of Verna Flogge.

Classic Memories

HOLIDAY SHOPPING AT RAY'S PLACE

A favorite pastime of mine is to arrive at Ray's and see what premium glasses are available along with a beverage like Labatt's, Guinness, Harp, etc. I select these and give them to friends and family as gifts. Very practical, as they love them and use them. They are thrilled because you can't get them at the brainless mall. They are practically collector items to friends who like beer, and they are usually free or maybe cost only a quarter extra. What better deal can you find? Enjoy your shopping and get a great, unique gift at no cost that the recipient really loves with a good cold beer for the shopper. *(Anon)*

THE CASH REGISTERS: ONE CLASSIC TO ANOTHER

Kristen Wilson and her grandfather Ed are two of the many people who love the classic cash registers at Ray's Place. Customers and employees alike get a kick out of the ringing sounds they make. And, when the place is really hopping (which is most of the time) and all the registers are ringing together, a sound emerges you will only find at Ray's.

My grandfather, Ed Helsel, fixed the cash registers at Ray's Place for many years. He would often bring me Ray's Place merchandise, such as T-shirts and sweatpants. I wore my T-shirts with pride! One year, when I was about 12 years old, my mom and I were vacationing in Fort Lauderdale, and I wore my Ray's Place T-shirt down to the pool. A young man wearing a Penn State T-shirt stopped me and told me that he had friends in college at Kent State and they had taken him there a few times. He thought it was so cute that such a young girl would be wearing a Ray's Place T-shirt! Grandpa always loved this story, and he always loved going to Ray's. He enjoyed talking to Charlie and the rest of the staff as well as customers who thought the old National Cash Registers were really neat! I sometimes got to go with him to Ray's Place, and that was so much fun. Dad loved showing me where he was working and was so proud to be at such a landmark. *(Wilson)*

Ray's famous 1940s vintage cash registers. Ray's Place features two of these downstairs and three upstairs. Photo by Mikala Pritts.

Many customers, including the author, wondered if the registers really worked or if they were there just for show. Be careful if you say that to Bob Dale who fixes the registers. Bob took over the cash register service business from his friend and mentor Ed Helsel. "I just love everything about them. Everyone loves them because they take them back in time," says Bob. Bob and Ed both worked many years for National Cash Register, which was founded and based in Dayton, Ohio. Since the registers are vintage 1940, some customers wonder where the parts will come from in the future. Bob advises, "I collect these classic registers as well as service them. I have about 800 of them!" Sounds like the cash registers are at Ray's Place to stay.

SEPTEMBER 11, 2001

Most of us remember where we were on Tuesday 9-11 when the World Trade Towers tumbled. One group of KSU history graduate students made some history of their own at Ray's that day.

My most poignant memory from Ray's is probably from September 11, 2001. At 9:00 that morning, I entered the Bowman Hall auditorium to assist with a recent U.S. history class; when the doors opened at 10:30 A.M., we were shocked to find that the current world had changed under our noses while we were talking about the past. After several hours of trying to keep up with news developments and individually dealing with the enormity of the day's events, a handful of graduate history students decided to meet upstairs at Ray's to talk about the past, present, and future and what it all meant. Aside from one guy sitting by himself at the bar, we had the place to ourselves—the only time I can remember that happening at Ray's, regardless of the time of day. Despite (or perhaps because of) the horror of that day, I'm sure on some level we ended up at Ray's because we thought of it as a refuge from the problems of the world, whatever their source or scope. Thinking back to talking about life and the world over a few pitchers of beer that night, there is no other place I would rather have been. *(Cary, '02)*

TOY NIGHT

I remember that on Wednesday evenings, Ray's Place gave out a trinket "toy" to all who entered between certain times. My roommate and I would enter the bar, get our toy, and begin mingling with our friends. We often ordered our favorite drink, the "Futher Mucker." The bathrooms were . . . um . . . less than desirable, but with each passing sip of our drinks, we noticed that less and less. Twenty years later, my roomie and I still talk of our fun evenings at Ray's and we plan to visit for lunch this summer! *(Cox, '92)*

Ray's has advertised for almost 70 years in KSU's student newspaper, *Daily Kent Stater,* starting with this ad on February 4, 1955.

RAY'S

STUDENT SPECIAL EACH DAY

RAY'S

OVEN HOT PIZZA

RAY'S

135 Franklin

Toy Night was Wednesday evening and was initiated by Charlie Thomas in the early 1980s. It ran for about 20 years and usually offered novelty items. Some of the various toys awarded on Toy Night included kazoos, noisemakers, toy cars, mini decks of cards, fake noses and mustaches, creepy crawlers, hairy spiders, jumping frogs, action figures, and finger puppets. For many customers, the toys they got at Ray's still hold considerable nostalgic value.

SINGIN' IN THE RAY'S

I was a member of the Collegiates Fraternity barbershop quartet. We won campus-wide honors for our extraordinary performances! We often practiced at Ray's Place. We called it Rocky's then. If not for the large quantities of Stroh's Bohemian beer, our quartet probably would have sounded more like the Andrews Sisters. Those old wooden booths have many tunes ringing in their timbers. Many students have passed through the doors since then, but not many of them won the quartet contests on campus with the vocal cord lubricant purchased at Ray's Place. *(Fichter '57, '64)*

I came to Kent right out of the army in 1959. I was a member of the Collegiates and was on both sides of Ray's bar, as a customer and as an employee. I met my wife there and many good friends. *(Weaver '63)*

I remember coming to Ray's after a particularly long night and hearing "Don't Stop Believing" start playing. Within 10 seconds, the entire bar was singing this song together at 2 A.M. It was a special moment that I won't soon forget. *(A. Goldberg)*

Ray's had the best jukebox selection in town with a half dozen each from Bruce Springsteen and Todd Rundgren. They also had a gem from Old Blue Eyes. Many a Thursday, Friday, and Saturday night after last call, my roommate at the time, Harold Weller, would stand on a table in the middle of the place and sing "My Way" to the crowd. *(Watson, '76)*

· ·

When the beer starts going down good I get the urge to start singing. I'm a
pretty good singer as long as the people listening have had one more pint
than me. (Anon)

RAY'SED AT RAY'S

· ·

In the mid '80s when we of the baby boomer generation were starting to
have kids and still wanted a place to gather and socialize, we all picked
Ray's for a variety of reasons: location, warm atmosphere, and most of us
were KSU alums. Three to four couples with our kids would meet in the
upstairs "nonsmoking pit" as we called it and enjoy a great meal and cold
beers with great servers (many of whom became friends to us over the
years). We would give the kids a roll of quarters to play the video games after dinner, and we would really enjoy our time together as new parents. We
are all nearly 60 years old now and still go to Ray's regularly and often with
our adult children who were "Raised at Ray's" and aren't really showing any
post-traumatic stress because of it! *(Duffy)*

· ·

I love going to Ray's because they have so many great import beers. I like
to do some mixing . . . like putting some Guinness on top of Harp or even
Smithwicks. The bartenders cook 'em up just right. I had a half-n-half once
and some couple sitting next to me at the bar asked what I was drinking. I
said . . . liquid art. *(Anon)*

You can buy a cheeseburger at Ray's, but you can't buy a beer at McDonald's.

Mo-Fos and Futher Muckers

Most restaurants have distinctive items that become closely associated with them over time. These are sometimes referred to as signature items—the sandwich, dessert, drink, or other menu item that the satisfied customer will recommend to the uninitiated. The customers at Ray's Place each have a number of these—like Gertie's chili, Sun Stix, or wings—but the two that stand out on most customers' lists are the Mo-Fo and the Futher Mucker. For almost 40 years, customers have been ordering up this sandwich and drink (not necessarily together). Both products were named by owners in the mid-1970s who wanted to expand customer options.

"When I think of Ray's I think of the Mo-Fo," says chef Michael Symon of the Food Network. Simon, known as Iron Mike, selected the sandwich on his "Best Thing I Ever Ate" segment. This comes from a successful restaurant entrepreneur who owns burger places! The ingredients are just about anything you can think of to put on a burger. Basically it's a bacon and mushroom double cheeseburger without the kitchen sink. More Mo-Fo info can be found on the Ray's Place website. The rumor is that the name Mo-Fo is a short version of "mo' fo' yo' money."

> 18. Total number of beers, including bottles and tap, upstairs and downstairs?

. . . .

We had gone to a restaurant in West Virginia to eat at a place featured on the Food Network. My husband had seen the Mo-Fo featured on the show as well. We decided to go there as well. So after lunch we drove to Ray's Place in Kent for the Mo-Fo sandwich. We went to both places on the same day. The staff was great and the burger was just as good—at least my husband said it was, and he was the one who ate it. What a great experience. (Bougourd)

The drink most often associated with Ray's Place is the Futher Mucker, a citrus-based adult beverage featuring a variety of distilled liquids. It's also rumored to have a secret ingredient, though no employee will confirm or deny the rumor or reveal the secret. It's quite popular at customer reunions, both large and small, and is seen by some customers as part of the 21st birthday rite of passage, as the following customer testifies:

Turning 21 and legally being able to drink "Futher Muckers" was a dream come true. What I remember most was waking up the morning after I had drank one or two for the first time and seeing my clothes thrown about my room and wondering how the heck I got home and how I got my clothes off! *(Bridgeman)*

Next time you're at Ray's Place you may very well hear a customer say, "I'll go with the Mo-Fo and a Futher Mucker." Or is it the other way around? The employees at Ray's Place have served many, many Mo-Fos and Futher Muckers over the years.

19. How many foreign beers are usually in stock?

Gertie's been making chili longer than Wendy's has been a franchise

Only at Ray's Place

It seems like there are some events and experiences that only happen at a place like Ray's. The following unique stories illustrate the point.

NICKNAMES FOR ALL

Mike D'Alessandro has worked at Ray's practically forever. Many years ago, a customer thought it odd that, with a last name like D'Alessandro, that his first name was Mike, so he started calling him Guido. Mike was less than pleased with this and commented about it to Charlie Thomas and other employees. To cheer him up, they all started calling him Guido, and to this day most people think his name really is Guido. Even his wife will ask for Guido when she calls Ray's to talk with him!

Ray's Place is famous for the nicknames given to employees and customers. In some cases, the origin of the nickname is known. In others, no one wants to know the origin.

Here are some nicknames given to employees:

Big Chris—long-time manager, origin of this one is pretty clear
The Bomb—aka The Blond Bombshell
Chucky—employee resembling a character from the movie *Ferris Bueller's Day Off*
Cowboy
Dumb Dave—he was dumb
Super Dumb Dave—dumber yet
Lenny
Meatball—uncanny resemblance to a ball of meat
Oatmeal
Opie—employee resembling a young Ron Howard
Papa Cool—Pat Stritch, manager in the '70s and '80s
Pooger—Pat Watson, long-time manager
Pooger Deuce—Pat Watson's nephew
Ray Man and Rae Woman—employee and girlfriend both named Ray
Shaggy—employee who resembled the Scooby Do character
Spider—two actually, one guy and one girl. Spiderman and Spiderwoman?

Super Pretty—customer once referred to this employee as Super Pretty

Tin—short for Kristin

And, some customer nicknames:

Basketball Jones—middle-aged guy from the '80s who carried a basketball under his shirt

Circle Lady—woman from the '80s who would come in, circle the bar twice, and leave

The Family—Sunday regulars

The Happy Family—another group of regulars but nowhere near as happy as The Family

Geek Squad—Tuesday regulars. Cool geeks.

Hamburglars—nice church group that came in weekly and ordered hamburgers

Jay-Z—no explanation needed on this one

The Mayor—aka Mayor of Crazytown

Moto

Put-in-Bay Johnny—looked like he belonged on this touristy Ohio island and had the tan to prove it

Rockin' Robin—quite a talented musician

Seven and Seven John—always drank a Seven and Seven. Occasionally his false teeth would fall out if he had too much to drink.

Spring Break Dennis

Tar Man

Time Bomb—orders a beer but never says another word . . . ever

T-Shirt Tom—ran a local T-shirt shop

Thanks to the Ray's Place managers, employees, and Tom Creech for generating the list.

· ·
Memories of Ray's? All I ever remember is going in. *(Anon)*

Lyle Alzado, an all-pro defensive end for the Cleveland Browns and other NFL teams visited Ray's Place from time to time. On one visit to Ray's, Lyle was caught dancing on the bar. After getting down from the bar, Alzado sheepishly told the owner at the time, Charlie Thomas, "They made me do it."

CHARLIE SAYS

Stop dancing and get down from the bar

I was out of money and needed a cosigner at the bank. Rocky came through and allowed me to finish the year. Without his help I would have had to drop out. He and Andy were helpful in so many ways. It was not just a place to eat and drink (which we did) but a place to go and be with friends. *(Childress)*

When I was hired on as the new chef, I was politely told, "Gertie's chili stays the same." Right. *(Chef Paone)*

One year at the local Christmas party, Sparky and I won the trip to Toronto, which was the big Kahuna prize that year. We had an amazing time. Ray's used to plan an annual Browns game trip—and a crazy bus ride to the stadium. I cannot fathom any restaurateur or bar owner that I have worked for who would ever go to these lengths to appreciate their employees. That Charlie Ray is a very rare jewel indeed. *(Bando, '89)*

I was working back in the late '70s and a guy brought a baby skunk in telling us it was too young to spray. Wrong! The skunk let out a spray right at closing time. Absolutely the fastest last call closing we ever had! *(Swan)*

The Ramones wanted to visit Ray's after playing a show at KSU. A limo pulled up and the driver asked how they could get in. I showed him the end of the line with all the people waiting to enter and commented "right there, along with everyone else"—much to the delight of all those waiting in line. They went elsewhere apparently. *(Watson)*

One cold November night a guy had had a bit too much to drink and was getting rowdy—actually broke one of our chairs, which got a quick response from the bartenders and managers. He ran out the door as they chased him and jumped the fence next to the train station. He ran across the tracks and apparently didn't know there was a second lower set of tracks about 20 feet down. After crashing on them he managed to get up and run toward the river. He jumped in and started swimming to avoid the guys chasing him but didn't realize the cops were on the scene by this time. The cops saw him swimming and went to the west side of the river bank to meet him. Unlucky night for him all the way around. The rumor was the guy's last name was actually Fish, and *The Record-Courier* ran a story with the headline reading something like "Fish Finds River Too Cold." *(Loudin)*

Entertainer Drew Carey has made a few famous visits to Ray's Place and is known for his generosity. After buying drinks for the bar one night he said he wanted to leave a 300 percent tip because he had never left that big of a tip before. Since the bar bill was almost $1,000, I told him a 300 percent tip would be $3,000! He said, "Screw it . . . go ahead. It's great to be a millionaire." *(Watson)*

20. What can you get by presenting your identification to a bartender on your birthday?

I enjoyed doing cartwheels on the bar at closing time. *(Anon)*

"You can pick your friends but not your family" is a familiar quote but not true when it comes to Ray's Place. It is amazing how a simple college bar can stir up nostalgia with everyone who has experienced it. I'd like to say I met my husband, Mario, there—that would make a great story—but I did fall in love with him over beer and Pat Powers's famous gin and tonics that made you talk loud and drink more gin. Yes, I have danced on the bars and tables and I was known for my lipstick kisses back in the day, but I wouldn't trade a moment for all the good friends and good times. When Charlie's wife, Diane, turned 60, many of us "old-timers" sat around a long table upstairs at Ray's. When I looked around the table at all the familiar faces, I recognized that we were a family. It was like an ideal Thanksgiving dinner with a loving family of friends. I will always be grateful for the man, Charlie Thomas, buying a little bar named Ray's Place and making it really a place to go home to. *(Wargo, '80, '05)*

71

21. What year did the moose first appear over the bar at Ray's?

The biggest and baddest wings in town

Chronology of Ray's Place

Vanetta "Gertie" Gritton, right front, and fellow employee ca. 1960. Gertie was a fixture at Ray's for 40 years. Photo courtesy of Charlie Thomas.

Rocky, left, and Andy Flogge in 1938. Photo courtesy of Al Flogge.

1863—A three-story building is built on Franklin Avenue in Kent, Ohio. Originally a hotel called the Central Hotel, it is later called the Collins House. Comedian and actor W. C. Fields once stayed at the Central Hotel while performing at the Kent Opera House. It is reported he left his suitcase as room payment since he had no money to pay his bill.

1937—Ray Salitore opens Ray's Place restaurant, converting a former drugstore. Ray caters mainly to railroad workers and travelers, war veterans, and local residents.

1945—Vanetta "Gertie" Gritton starts work at Ray's Place. Gertie worked for all four owners. She had a dog named Snoopy. She once commented to a new owner, "I come with the place." A portrait of Gertie hangs near the kitchen where her secret chili recipe is still used today.

1946—Ray Salitore sells to Rocky and Andy Flogge. Most of the Flogge family is involved in the business in one way or another. Verna Flogge, Andy's wife, introduces pizza in 1946.

1946—Rocky and Andy introduce television to Ray's Place. Customers watch sporting events making Ray's Place one of the first bars in America to televise sports.

1954—Ray Salitore passes away.

1968—Third floor of building is demolished after a fire.

Charlie Thomas leans on the bar under Ray's famous moose in 1983. Photo by Lew Stamp. Photo courtesy of the *Akron Beacon Journal*.

In 1992 the *Record Courier* ran a story about transforming the upstairs of Ray's Place from Mother's Junction to Ray's Upstairs. Photo courtesy of the *Record-Courier*.

1975—Rocky and Andy sell to Buddy and Mary LoCicero and Tom and Jay Shaw after 29 years of ownership. The new owners come up with new products, such as a 49-cent breakfast, the Mo-Fo sandwich, and the Futher Mucker drink, and introduced imported beer.

1977—Shaw and LoCicero create a band bar upstairs named Mother's.

1978—Shaw and LoCicero sell to Charles "Charlie" Thomas in December.

1980—Charlie changes name of Mother's to Mother's Junction.

1980—Moose first appears over the bar at Ray's. It may have been connected to a promotion for Moosehead beer. Some regular customers form a group called the Mooseherd.

1985—Gertie retires from Ray's after 40 years. She passes away in April 1990.

1992—Charlie converts Mother's Junction to Ray's Upstairs. IMMY Award from Kent Chamber of Commerce presented to Charlie for the upstairs improvement.

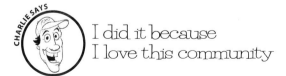

I did it because I love this community

1992—*Northern Ohio Live* ranks Ray's as the No. 1 bar in northeast Ohio.

In 2003 Charlie Thomas was named Small Business Person of the Year by the Kent Area Chamber of Commerce (KACC). Pictured here are Charlie and his wife, Diane, at the KACC banquet. Photo by Dan Smith. Courtesy of the KACC.

1998—Ray's downstairs gets a total makeover, restoring the front windows to their original look.

2003—Charlie Thomas is recognized as Small Business Person of the Year by the Kent Chamber of Commerce.

2010—Charlie establishes entrepreneurship scholarship at Kent State University's College of Business Administration.

2012—Ray's celebrates 75 years in business.

2013—*Meet Me at Ray's* is published by Black Squirrel Books, an imprint of Kent State University Press.

Ray's Phrases*

- Where townies meet with students
- Early old-fashioned flavor of the original Ray's has always been maintained
- A really friendly place
- Like a bar you'd find in the French Quarter of New Orleans or on the banks of the River Seine
- It's almost an institution
- A favorite meeting spot
- A veritable Franklin Avenue fixture
- Inflated quality without the inflated price
- A home away from home
- Well-worn bastion of conviviality
- They always welcome business people, students, garbage collectors, janitors, and rock 'n' rollers in general
- Downstairs is old charm and upstairs is new charm
- Tradition-laden popular pub
- It's not an ordinary bar even though it looks like one

- Franklin Avenue stalwart
- Where hustlers meet to hustle the hustlers
- Nationally renowned
- The place to start and end
- The place for the not-too-picky eater
- Venerable Kent landmark
- Kent's most popular restaurant
- Kent's long-standing restaurant
- No. 1 bar in northeast Ohio
- One of *Playboy's* best 100 college bars in the nation
- A really friendly place to meet with friends and to make new ones
- Iconic alehouse
- A bar where you can take your parents and your grandparents
- A heckuva place to eat
- It's more than an institution, it's a religion

Taken from media stories about Ray's Place over the years.

So Why Does It Work?

What is it about Ray's Place that commands such loyalty and affection from both customers and employees? I often refer to Ray's Place as the Harley-Davidson of college bars. Like the motorcycle, it has created a fiercely loyal following of people who view it almost as a lifestyle. From the Ray's Gang to the Mooseherd, Ray's Place customers are fans for life. And employee commitment is just as evident in many ways.

After writing and researching this book and learning from the hundreds of experiences of employees and customers, I believe I have an inside perspective on why Ray's Place has been so successful. I think it all boils down to three things: the customers, the employees, and the owners.

THE CUSTOMERS

The loyal and long-time customers feel a strong sense of ownership about Ray's Place. They feel like it truly is their place. Some sit in the same place each time they go, some carve their initials in the booths, many take pictures of the place with their friends while visiting, some treasure their toys from Toy Night, some form little clubs, and still others hug friends and employees each time they visit. Whether the connection to Ray's Place is as a Kent resident or an association with KSU, everyone who frequents Ray's shares this feeling of ownership.

The customers vary at Ray's Place pretty much based on the time of day, the day of the week, a special occasion, or a particular sporting event. At times it's a lunch place for working folks, at other times it's a family dinner place, and still other times a popular happy hour spot. It can also be a meeting place and a sports bar. Sometimes it's all of these at the same time! It all depends on which group of customers is there and why.

Weekday lunch hours are packed with university professors, local professionals, and blue-collar workers. It's almost impossible to get a table on Friday and Saturday from 5 to 9 P.M. as they're all taken with students, families, and working people winding down from the week. Late weekday evenings are frequented mainly by students looking to meet and party with their friends. Saturday and Sunday afternoons are packed with sports fans watching any number of different sporting events. Although the restaurant is still the same place, it takes on a different flavor due to the customers there at any given time. A customer once described Ray's as "the place you can take your parents or your grandparents."

Alma mater is a Latin phrase that translates to "nourishing mother." Graduates of schools and universities refer to their school as alma mater because educational institutions, especially colleges and universities, provide nourishment similar to that of a mother. Our college experiences stay with us for life, and in some respects they define our lives. In addition to the classes, the social life, roommates, the library, the sporting events, the parties, and all the other things that make up the college experience, the town itself becomes another aspect of the "nourishing mother."

I think customers return to Ray's Place because it nourishes them. It nourishes them in mind, body, spirit, and soul. It is evident in the stories they have shared. Ray's Place has made changes over the years, but in many ways and for many customers Ray's Place remains a familiar place despite the changes. The menu is pretty much the same as you remember and so are all the employees. Gertie's chili tastes the same. The booths, the bar, the Moose, the shot wheel, and the cash registers are consistent in the customer's mind. We're all familiar with the phrase "you can't go home again." Well, at Ray's Place in Kent, Ohio, you can go home again. And, you can go home as often as you wish.

Another thought about the unique customer vibe at Ray's Place relates to the rapid pace of change we've seen in our society, particularly in the last 10 to 15 years. People can now have thousands of online "friends" yet still be alone. Technology is both connecting and separating us at the same time. At Ray's Place, the customers are talking to each other and to the employees. People laugh together, joke around, tease, and hug each other. And, occasionally you might even see a teary eye or two.

Ray's Place is a very friendly and sociable place. You rarely see people texting or talking on cell phones. The customers are there celebrating with their friends. There will be people of all ages and from all walks of life enjoying their time together. You will also see lots of families together. I often think about the children who are there and that the parents they are sitting with probably also sat with their parents some years ago. I imagine those kids will one day sit at Ray's with their kids. The cycle continues.

Ray's has a truly unique workforce. Many of the managers, servers, and kitchen staff have worked there for years. Some have worked there over 30 years, which is rare in the small business world today. Ray's has a management team with an average 25 years of employment. The serving and kitchen staff number about 40 with an average employment of 10 years. I can only conclude that full-time employees and managers must be receiving a decent wage and benefits package or they would most likely leave. But there's more to it than just compensation. You can see their dedication to Ray's and the owners in the stories they have shared in this book. Also, stories shared by employees who worked for previous owners have a similar affection in their stories.

Every Ray's employee begins his or her experience as an employee by checking IDs at the door. That's where you learn about the customer. It's also a bit of an initiation and a baptism into the Ray's Place family of employees that numbers around 900, past and present, for the current owner. If you really want to work at Ray's you have to prove it by working the door. This gives all employees a common experience and starting point. It is one of the reasons that an esprit de corps shows up in their work. Ray's is a place where employees set up fundraisers to help a customer or fellow employee when an illness strikes. It's a place where employees chip in and buy a present for a five-year-old who is celebrating a birthday with her family at Ray's Place.

Another factor that builds cooperation is the pooling of tips. No bartender or server is assigned to a specific table, section, or shift. In many restaurants, this can become a source of friction because the shifts and sections you work often determine how much tip money you will earn. When tips are pooled and equally divided, this tension is removed. This also has all staff serving all customers. A server may take your drink order and a different server might bring the drink to your booth or table. A different server or perhaps even a bartender might bring your food to the table, and someone else might handle your checkout. As a customer, you get the feeling that everyone working at Ray's is serving you. This creates a great atmosphere for everyone.

Ray's employees learn a great deal about the restaurant business and working in general as a result of working there. Many former employees have shared stories about how their work experience at Ray's has helped them throughout their work and personal lives. Make no mistake—working at Ray's is hard work. Anyone who has ever worked in the restaurant business will testify to that. But at Ray's, even though the employees are working hard and really hustling, there is still a positive energy throughout the place. A business education from Ray's lasts a lifetime.

The employees also stay in touch with each other. Ray's has employee reunions periodically with dozens of former employees, many of whom met their spouses while working at Ray's, returning to relive their experiences. It's a good bit like a Homecoming. It's a lot like visiting the alma mater.

THE OWNERS

So what is the engine that drives Ray's Place? The heartbeat of the whole place for more than 75 years? The owners. All four owners have left their mark on Ray's. The warmth and affection customers and employees display for the owners just jumps off the pages and pictures in this book. Lincoln Filene, a major player in the early development of department stores, said, "Employees learn how to treat customers from the way they are treated by their managers." The owners of Ray's Place have set the example consistently since 1937.

The owners create a place where people enjoy working. It's a place where an owner might give a nickname to an employee. I've been frequenting Ray's Place for more than 25 years and only found out by writing this book that Guido is a nickname for Mike D'Alessandro, a 27-year veteran employee. Most customers (and probably a few employees as well) think Mike's real name is Guido. If there is a secret to the success of Ray's Place, this is it. The owners truly have been and truly are people oriented.

The owners were and are also very good business people. After all, it is their livelihood as well as secure employment for many employees.

We try to keep changing
while remaining the same

All of the owners were ahead of the curve in their own way. The number of firsts identified throughout this book (first bar to televise sports, first pizza, first import beer, etc.) are indications of the business savvy of each owner. Hockey hall-of-famer Wayne Gretzky is credited with the phrase "skate to where the puck is going." The owners of Ray's have done some pretty good skating for more than three-quarters of a century.

Because of the customers, the employees, and the owners, Ray's Place remains all the good things it was when Ray Salitore started it all those years ago. It's still the same friendly place where all sorts of people meet, greet, and eat together. It's a place where each visit seems like another reunion.

FUTURE STORIES?

We are still interested in your stories about Ray's Place. If you have a story you would like to be included in a future edition, submit it on the Ray's Place website: www.RaysPlaceKent.com

Ray's Your I.Q.

All answers appear somewhere in the book as well as on page 82.

1. Who came up with the idea of the shot wheel?
2. Who came up with the name for the Futher Mucker drink?
3. Who named the Mo-Fo ?
4. What did S.O.B. stand for in a past sandwich menu item?
5. Who was Gertie?
6. What brand and vintage are the cash registers?
7. Was the upstairs phone booth ever in use at Ray's?
8. What is really going on in the Spaghetti Feast advertisement?
9. Who was Stereo Chuck?
10. How many Ray's collector pint glasses are distributed during a typical Homecoming?
11. What is current owner Charlie Thomas's middle name?
12. What brand of television was the first one at Ray's in 1946?
13. Which Ray's employee has the longest tenure?
14. Guido is a nickname for what Ray's manager?

Spaghetti Night remains popular, especially with hungry college students. Advertisement in the *Daily Kent Stater*, May 2, 1992.

15. Who gave Guido his nickname?
16. Buddy LoCicero, a Ray's Place owner in the 1970s, was in a band called the Measles. What instrument did he play?
17. Who painted the downstairs murals?
18. Total number of beers, including bottles and tap, upstairs and downstairs?
19. How many foreign beers are usually in stock?
20. What can you get by presenting your identification to a bartender on your birthday?
21. What year did the moose first appear over the bar at Ray's?

Ray's Your I.Q. Answers

1. Former employee Jeff Kean came up with the idea and Steve Harris constructed it
2. Buddy LoCicero
3. Buddy, but party line is that the name is short for mo' fo' yo' money
4. Smoked Oyster Bacon
5. Vanetta Gritton who worked at Ray's for all four owners
6. National Cash Register, 1940s
7. Yes, until 2002; originally built in 1992 by Tom Creech and Tom McCarthy
8. Ad by Heinrich Kley shows people eating spaghetti off a man
9. name used by Charlie Thomas when selling stereos out of the trunk of his car in late 1960s
10. 500
11. Ray
12. Muntz
13. Tom Creech since 1979
14. Mike D'Alessandro
15. a customer; the nickname was reinforced by Charlie Thomas and other employees
16. the drums
17. Ken Muntzenmayer
18. 224
19. 77
20. a free drink by spinning the shot wheel
21. 1980

The Title Contest

Susan O'Connor, my bride, came up with the idea that we should have a contest to title the book . . . Great idea, we thought, so that's what we did. We had 29 submissions for the book title. Thanks to all who participated.

We assembled a secret crack team of book title novices and locked them in a room at an undisclosed location. They took the 29 suggestions and bandied them about for what seemed like an eternity. Actually, it was a pretty taxing task as there were many great suggestions.

Eventually, they selected a title for the book. The selected title, *Meet Me at Ray's,* was actually offered by two people; Mike Kaschak and Dan Karp. Mike is a two-time KSU graduate ('95 and '02) and currently works as a school administrator in the Akron-Canton area. Mike's wife, Stacia, is also a multiple-time KSU graduate. Mike's story about Ray's appears on page 53. Dan works as a creative director for the KSU marketing and communication division. His wife, Merri, is also a KSU graduate. After graduation, they lived in Chicago and then Berea, Ohio, before coming full swing and returning to KSU and Ray's. Dan's Ray's story appears on page 30.

A few of the other highly ranked title suggestions included *Flashbacks: The Story of Ray's, Ray's Remains the Same,* and *Ray's of Our Lives.* In the end we chose *Meet Me at Ray's* because it sums up the friendly meeting place that we have come to know and love. It's a phrase that has doubtless crossed the lips of thousands of Ray's Place friends over the decades. We thank Mike and Dan for the title suggestion and hope they feel immortalized.